FEATURES

SUMMER 2023 • NUMBER 36

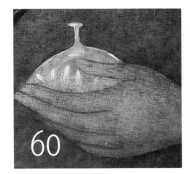

Plough

DEPARTMENTS

WEB EXCLUSIVES

Read these articles at *plough.com/web36*.

Plough
ANOTHER LIFE IS POSSIBLE

EDITOR: Peter Mommsen
SENIOR EDITORS: Shana Goodwin, Maria Hine, Maureen Swinger, Sam Hine, Susannah Black Roberts
EDITOR-AT-LARGE: Caitrin Keiper
BOOKS AND CULTURE EDITOR: Joy Marie Clarkson
POETRY EDITOR: A. M. Juster
DESIGNERS: Rosalind Stevenson, Miriam Burleson
CREATIVE DIRECTOR: Clare Stober
COPY EDITORS: Wilma Mommsen, Priscilla Jensen
FACT CHECKER: Suzanne Quinta
MARKETING DIRECTOR: Trevor Wiser
UK EDITION: Ian Barth
CONTRIBUTING EDITORS: Leah Libresco Sargeant, Brandon McGinley, Jake Meador
FOUNDING EDITOR: Eberhard Arnold (1883–1935)

Plough Quarterly No. 36: Money
Published by Plough Publishing House, ISBN 978-1-63608-084-0
Copyright © 2023 by Plough Publishing House. All rights reserved.

EDITORIAL OFFICE
151 Bowne Drive
Walden, NY 12586
T: 845.572.3455
info@plough.com

SUBSCRIBER SERVICES
PO Box 8542
Big Sandy, TX 75755
T: 800.521.8011
subscriptions@plough.com

United Kingdom
Brightling Road
Robertsbridge
TN32 5DR
T: +44(0)1580.883.344

Australia
4188 Gwydir Highway
Elsmore, NSW
2360 Australia
T: +61(0)2.6723.2213

Plough Quarterly (ISSN 2372-2584) is published quarterly by Plough Publishing House, PO Box 398, Walden, NY 12586.
Individual subscription $36 / £24 / €28 per year.
Subscribers outside of the United States and Canada pay in British pounds or euros.
Periodicals postage paid at Walden, NY 12586 and at additional mailing offices.
POSTMASTER: Send address changes to Plough Quarterly, PO Box 8542, Big Sandy, TX 75755.

Front cover: Mark Wagner, *Of Spiders and Flies*, currency on panel, 2013. Used by permission.
Inside front cover: Ohara Koson, *Leaping Salmon*. Public domain.
Back cover: Daniel Bonnell, *Saint Francis, Dove and the Wolf*. Used by permission.

ABOUT THE COVER

It's easy to become entangled in the complex web that money weaves around our decisions, interactions, and relationships. The artist Mark Wagner crafted this issue's cover art, entitled *Of Spiders and Flies*, out of US currency.

LETTERS

READERS RESPOND

Readers respond to *Plough*'s Spring 2023 issue, "Pain and Passion." Send letters to *letters@plough.com.*

THE CHURCH AND EUTHANASIA

On Benjamin Crosby's "Ten Thousand Gentle Killings": I am an Australian respiratory specialist and have end-of-life discussions with people most days of the week, usually with people dying of lung cancer or emphysema. In my home state euthanasia became legal eight weeks ago. In my health jurisdiction of 1.5 million people, fifteen have been supplied a lethal drug; nine have taken it to date. I would like first to acknowledge the feelings of those who think euthanasia may be appropriate in some situations; they are often influenced by watching a loved one die, one of life's most upsetting universal experiences.

In Australian opinion polls there is fairly wide support for euthanasia; by next year it will be available in all states. As a doctor I have found that the debate over euthanasia has reflected a very limited understanding of the dying process and the nature and scope of palliative care; here the debate has been driven by activist politicians and right-to-die groups which often sensationalize extreme and uncommon examples of suffering.

Most of these cases do not reflect what I have seen in my twenty-five years as a doctor – I would suggest that few people in Australia die in the extreme pain that is so often given as a reason for legalizing

euthanasia. Evidence from other countries suggests most who take the option do so because of loss of independence and fear of being a burden to others. My observation of death is different – when I ring family members to offer condolences on the death of a loved one, they often tell me of a peaceful death and express gratitude for the palliative care and respiratory nurses who made that possible.

Some nurses have told me they support euthanasia because they don't want to watch people die. I remember hearing something like this in medical school thirty years ago – a psychiatrist noted that often arguments for euthanasia are complicated by families' fear not only of patients' dying but of how difficult it is for loved ones to deal with this suffering. To me, this evidence suggests that in choosing euthanasia because they perceive themselves to be a burden to others, patients are suggesting they can't deal with their loved ones' suffering as well.

As a Catholic doctor who is opposed to abortion, I assumed my many medical friends who disagree with me on this issue would also disagree with me on euthanasia. However, the majority want nothing to do with it; many atheist doctors are vehemently opposed to euthanasia. We know what good palliative care and end-of-life planning can offer. We know we often get prognoses wrong – I have many patients coming to my clinic who should have been dead years ago. We also know that the great majority of those who took the euthanasia option would have had peaceful deaths with good palliative care. When

this does not happen, it is far more likely due to health-care disparities than a lack of euthanasia availability.

Dr. Andrew Burke, Brisbane, Australia

I am what some would define as a liberal Christian. I believe in a woman's control of her body and the right of an individual to end his or her own life when that life is beyond medical recovery. However, I also believe that these are very complex, profound, and personal moral issues that demand respectful exploration and self-examination. This does not happen often in today's world, and it does not happen at all without people like those writing in *Plough* pushing us to question and evaluate our values and beliefs.

Benjamin Crosby's article on Canada's experiment with euthanasia is a case in point. *Plough*'s articles on abortion as a method of eugenics is another. In each case, I have had to ponder, reconsider, and change.

David Crosson, San Francisco, California

My younger brother Jon died of cancer in his early twenties. It was painful to see a healthy, strong twenty-year-old turn into an emaciated skeleton in just eighteen months. I remember, near the end of his life, pleading with God that he would die quickly. It was almost unbearable to see him in pain and feel so helpless. I wondered whether it could be merciful to help someone die gently and sooner, to spare them that pain. Sparing those we love from pain is a natural and good instinct.

But sparing pain is not the only form love takes. Seeing people who have suffered painful things or have been forced to live with a disability, things I would never choose for myself, and yet have grown into compassionate, beautiful people, challenges me to reconsider. I hesitate to pronounce judgment when I am so afraid of pain and disability. But we must consider those who have suffered, and have transformed their pain into compassion; who have found a meaningful, satisfying life with disability, with pain. Not for the sake of argument alone, but to offer an alternative vision of what constitutes a worthy life, a valuable life, and a good life.

Perhaps this is the unique vocation of the church. Not to compel others to live as we think they should, nor condemning them when they don't, but offering an alternative vision, a better vision of what constitutes a meaningful life through how we value and care for each other. That is the ultimate question underlying euthanasia: What makes a life valuable, or worth living? Our best answer is not argument, but example. A more compelling, more beautiful, more meaningful way to live and value life. An irresistible vision, rather than an irrefutable one.

But what of terminal cases? Part of what compels me toward the Christian vision of life is that it takes death both more seriously, and more lightly. It frees us from the fear of death, and the fear of life. We can heartily affirm the goodness of life and death. To summarize Paul, to live is a joy because we can help others, and to die is to our advantage, because we go home to something even better.

Matthew Pound, Chiang Mai, Thailand

Tolstoy's "Death of Ivan Ilyich" seems very prescient on this issue and the way a medicalized vision of life and death warps our conception of what it means to live and die. Gerasim, to Ivan's shock, cares for him in the indignities of illness, saying, "We'll all be there someday." This vision isn't possible when late-life, illness, and death are relegated to the antiseptic rooms of hospitals. The greatest insight I've had into holy living and dying has been from caring for my own father, my grandmother, and another elderly woman in my home as they died. Those experiences have convicted me of my own responsibility to care for others in this fundamental human process and the desire to bear my own death when my time comes.

Chris Bonner, Tyler, Texas

Working as a nurse in ICU, I interact with death and dying frequently. The medical machine rolls on until someone says stop. When a person or family makes the decision to stop (feeding, hydration, ventilation) we assist with medication for pain or anxiety. When we rely on modern medicine but have faith as backup, is it OK to choose not to be resuscitated? Death, childbirth, and old age can be painful; how much should believers rely on the benefits of science rather than accepting discomfort?

Jason Sannes-Venhuizen, Frazee, Minnesota

ENGRAVED ON THE HEART

On Lisabeth Button's "Letters from a Vanishing Friend": I was moved by Ms. Button's biography of her improbable friendship with Ellen, the childhood friend eventually afflicted with Alzheimer's disease.

A detail that struck me was how Ellen might have been considered "lost" only to write a letter that was insightful and poignant.

I serve weekly as a Eucharistic minister to Catholic hospital patients wishing to receive communion.

Recently a note explained that a patient suffered from dementia, so any conversation would not be possible. Indeed, my greeting was received with a blank stare and no evidence of recognition or purpose.

Nonetheless, I decided to proceed and improvise as the spirit led me. As soon as the cadences of that ancient rite began, the old man lit up. His part of every response and prayer was recited perfectly. It was as though this sacred information was engraved on his heart and found a way for him to give it voice one more time.

George E. Pence III, Salt Lake City, Utah

ABOUT US

Plough is published by the Bruderhof, an international community of families and singles seeking to follow Jesus together. Members of the Bruderhof are committed to a way of radical disciple-ship in the spirit of the Sermon on the Mount. Inspired by the first church in Jerusalem (Acts 2 and 4), they renounce private property and share everything in common in a life of nonviolence, justice, and service to neighbors near and far. There are twenty-nine Bruderhof settlements in both rural and urban locations in the United States, England, Germany, Australia, Paraguay, South Korea, and Austria, with around 3000 people in all. To learn more or arrange a visit, see the community's website at *bruderhof.com*.

Plough features original stories, ideas, and culture to inspire faith and action. Starting from the conviction that the teachings and example of Jesus can transform and renew our world, we aim to apply them to all aspects of life, seeking common ground with all people of goodwill regardless of creed. The goal of *Plough* is to build a living network of readers, contributors, and practitioners so that, as we read in Hebrews, we may "spur one another on toward love and good deeds."

Plough includes contributions that we believe are worthy of our readers' consideration, whether or not we fully agree with them. Views expressed by contributors are their own and do not necessarily reflect the editorial position of *Plough* or of the Bruderhof communities. ➤

NO GRIEF WITHOUT LOVE

On the PloughCast episode, "C. S. Lewis and the Problem of Pain": As I wrote in "Another Grief Observed" for *Plough* several years ago, in my experience, love was the only redeeming force in the midst of grief. Guided by love, friends did what they could and community softened the hardness of grief. Sharing it all, Victoria (my wife) and I love each other all the more. In the context of love, the experiences of profound sorrow, gratitude, and joy are not mutually exclusive. We can love without grief but we do not grieve without love, and I would rather live in a world with grief than in a world without love.

Larry A. Smith, Cortona, Italy

THE EMPTY HANDS

On Eduardo Galeano's "Communion of Empty Hands": I was moved to tears by your article and artwork of empty hands communion. I lived in Argentina during the dirty war in the seventies; Uruguay was also in the throes of dictatorship, prison, torture, and death. I remembered my friend who was the only survivor of a large group of university students who were tortured and killed. She was spared because the military realized that she was a US citizen.

The empty hands gave me an image of not knowing how to pray or what to pray and I found comfort in just offering my unknowing to the author of life itself, so that the One who does know all can work in the midst of the mystery that makes all things new.

Betty Puricelli, Toronto, Ontario

THE ONE WHO HELPS

On Elise Tegegne's "Foolish Generosity" on plough.com: I have worked on the streets of New York City's poorest neighborhoods for decades. Initially, I was like the author; I always looked away or only gave out money to get rid of a troublesome person. But with the passage of time I realized that nobody is a con. They are the desperate, impoverished, and broken among us who come to us in their need. So what if they ask for food money and then buy a cheap bottle of wine? Those few dollars relieve their pain for an hour or two. To judge the least among us for their desperation because they prefer cash to a pair of socks is kind of missing the message.

Lee Allen, Lewisboro, New York

Back in the 1970s, I was a homeless teenage runaway from a violent alcoholic family for two years, until I could get legal and get back in the normal world. And I did. Both being homeless and becoming non-homeless were very hard. There are a lot of reasons people end up on the streets, and a lot of reasons people beg for money. To this day, if someone asks me for money, I'll give it to them. I'd rather be taken for a sucker than be the one who doesn't help.

Eve Fisher, Sioux Falls, South Dakota ➤

The Mustard Seed Project

Amid the apartment blocks of Gotha, Germany, a small city mission welcomes its neighbors.

Since 2015, *Senfkorn Stadtteilmission* – "the mustard seed neighborhood mission" – has been experimenting with new ways of building community amid the monotonous apartment blocks of Gotha, in Germany's former East Zone. Its aim? To spread faith, hope, and love among the *Kirchenfernen* – those who are "far from the church." *Senfkorn* was started in 2015 by Lutheran pastor Michael Weinmann and his wife Christiane; in 2021 they were joined by Frank and Ute Paul, longtime intercultural workers in Argentina and members of OJC,

an intentional community south of Frankfurt. *Plough's* Chris Zimmerman spoke with Michael and Ute.

Plough: How do you do mission in Germany, a country that's been Christian for centuries?

Ute Paul: Only about 1 percent of the ten thousand residents in our neighborhood attend church. For most, religious services and faith are out of sight, out of mind – completely meaningless. So the challenge is great. But we are not running a mission program! We simply want to be present as Jesus-people and to trust that he is already here.

Michael Weinmann: "Mission" is a threadbare word; it implies that certain people have something to bring to others, who lack it. This has never been our approach. We see ourselves as participating in the much broader mission of God who, in Jesus, entered our world in order to love and reconcile it. That requires living among the people as part of an open, post-denominational community focused on the horizon – on the coming kingdom of God. Our name comes from a story Jesus told about a mustard seed, about this tiny little possibility of new life. It is easily overlooked; it is apparently meaningless. But once it takes root among the cracks in the

Frank Paul sits with a young visitor to the Mustard Seed Store, a community center.

concrete, it grows and grows, eventually providing shade and shelter for even the strangest birds!

Ute Paul: It is important for people to see their own ideas and suggestions being implemented. Our aim is to collaborate; to work toward viable, lovable daily interactions with those already living and working here; to nurture self-efficacy and confidence. It's *their* neighborhood!

What's the neighborhood like?

Ute Paul: The apartment blocks here were built in the 1980s, and there are still "original" residents, mostly elderly. Many moved away after the so-called "peaceful revolution" [of 1989] though. They were replaced by newer residents looking for affordable housing: low-income employees, welfare recipients, single mothers. There's been a steady influx of migrants too: from the Balkans, Eastern Europe, the Middle East and Africa, and most recently, Ukraine. Time and again, fear and prejudices lead to conflicts between these groups. Communication is a big problem.

What is a typical day?

Michael Weinmann: We make house visits, and when people stop us on the street, we try to listen to their concerns. Christiane, who is an art teacher, holds free painting sessions for children in a storefront. We use it for prayer and worship too, and for educational films, German classes, and roundtables. I also teach religion at a local school, and I regularly tell Bible stories to pupils from a nearby secular kindergarten.

Ute Paul: Our primary concern is building relationships with others, so we are always out and about on foot. We try to be attentive to "random" encounters: God can send someone your way at any time. Beyond that, we invite people to our store – to paint, hang out, or drink coffee. We also hold noon prayers, and a Bible discovery group – and, twice a month, a worship service. There's lively singing, storytelling, and opportunities for listening to one another. No two days are the same. We try to let the Spirit be our guide.

Tell me about the different people you interact with.

Ute Paul: It's a diverse crowd. So are the stories that come to light as we get to know them. Many have a deep desire to share. There are serious family dramas. Sometimes it's hard to deal with it all – my patience has its limits. We seem to move between two poles: the mistaken wish that people would change (which undercuts love and acceptance) and our faith in the "mustard seed" idea – our hope that they

might experience God's salvation in every area of their lives (which reminds us to wait for his working).

It's painful to be confronted with the despair, addictions, anger, powerlessness, and grief that define life for so many, whether single mothers, lonely senior citizens, traumatized teens, or simply the overworked – people of all ages. Maybe we are here so that we cannot run away from the pain, but have to hold it out, in hope, to God.

There are beautiful things, like the breakfast we host on Wednesdays. Everyone brought something to the first one, and we opened the door so that whoever wanted to come in off the square would feel welcome. There was chatter and laughter. It was so human, so simple. But the joy! A woman told me, "I've been looking forward to this all week." And then she thanked God.

Michael, you used to have a beautiful rectory in a nice neighborhood. What led you to move?

Michael Weinmann: I couldn't preach to others about Jesus and how he went out among the people while staying in my own comfort zone. Of course it's challenging. There are complex problems. A friend said, "You're moving to the Golan Heights!" – meaning a war zone. But we have to be careful not to stigmatize others with such characterizations. Then again, we are not trying to build up a congregation or parish in the traditional sense.

Many recent migrants to Germany are Muslim. How do they respond to you?

Michael Weinmann: Very positively. In fact, it's often Muslims who are most eager

The apartment blocks in Gotha-West.

to talk with us about faith. On the other hand, there are folks whose attitudes might be summed up with "Refugees not welcome!" Sometimes we find one of our windows broken.

Ute Paul: We want to live here as bridge-builders, which means cultivating friendship with people who open their doors to us. There is always so much we don't know. But at root, every human being wants to be met with respect. That sometimes means listening to their anxieties and not dismissing them. Fear dissipates when real encounters happen; we've seen that again and again.

My first day here, I met a young Syrian woman in the hallway; before long we were drinking coffee together. Her husband was skeptical. What did this German woman want with them? In the meantime, it's developed into a precious friendship; I'm studying Arabic with her and learning about the Muslims' deep reverence for God. I brought her roses during Ramadan. And she listens so attentively when I tell her stories about Jesus.

On the other hand, it's worrying how quickly fears of "foreign infiltration" can be politicized and instrumentalized. As Michael indicated, not everyone likes the fact that we welcome migrants.

What about the Christian aspect of your message? Are people even interested in religion?

Michael Weinmann: It's not about imposing abstract ideas on people. That's not why we're here. It's about a shared life. Of course, in a secular world, you have to keep asking yourself, "What do I really have to say?" And: "How do I say it?"

Ute Paul: Our experience is that everyone longs for community. This is the door! – no matter what age, no matter the situation. That's why, from the very beginning, we have been looking for a different way – one that takes that longing into account. A brand new way of being a church, of living our faith in everyday life, of nurturing trust through real relationships. That's what breaks down the walls that people put up to keep out God and the church, for whatever reason.

Young people, too, begin to ask deeper questions when their perspectives are taken seriously. The challenge is to find an understandable language for the message entrusted to us – the message of reconciliation, community, and joy.

Of course, the greatest impact is when people experience these things for themselves. An elderly lady we know was grieving the recent death of her mother when she ran into one of the teens who drops by our store, a young man who doesn't have it so easy himself. When she told him what she was going through, he spontaneously hugged her and comforted her. She was moved, but in the end, the encounter meant as much to the young man himself as to her – he was so amazed by the power of one small gesture. Because we invite people to share stories at our weekly meetings, this one spread. With each telling, it was as if the light grew stronger. ➤

Translated from the German by Chris Zimmerman.

Rhina Espaillat Poetry Award Winners

Congratulations to winner Jean L. Kreiling for her poem "*Claire de lune,*" and to finalists Matthew King for "Advent" and Midge Goldberg for "Argument of Periapsis," all published in the pages of this issue. The winners of *Plough*'s third annual poetry contest were announced at a livestreamed event with Rhina P. Espaillat and poetry editor A. M. Juster. The award is for a poem of not more than fifty lines that reflects Espaillat's lyricism, empathy, and ability to find grace in everyday events of life. The 2023 competition attracted over 900 poems.

Jean L. Kreiling is the author of three collections of poetry: *Shared History* (2022), *Arts & Letters & Love* (2018), and *The Truth in Dissonance* (2014). Her poems appear widely in print and online journals and in anthologies. Her work has been awarded the Frost Farm Prize for Metrical Poetry, the Great Lakes Commonwealth of Letters Sonnet Prize, the Plymouth Poetry Contest prize, and the *String Poet* Prize, among other honors. Kreiling is professor emeritus of music at Bridgewater State University and an associate poetry editor for *Able Muse: A Review of Poetry, Prose & Art*. She lives on the coast of Massachusetts. Her poem, "Claire de lune" appears on page 35.

Matthew King used to teach philosophy at York University in Toronto, Canada; he now lives in what Al Purdy called "the country north of Belleville," where he tries to grow things, counts birds, and takes pictures of flowers with bugs on them. He won the 2020/21 *FreeFall Magazine* poetry contest and was shortlisted in the 2023 Kim Bridgford Memorial Sonnet Contest, and has poems published or forthcoming in places such as *Rattle, Pulsebeat, Orchards Poetry Journal*, and *Best Canadian Poetry*. His poem, "Advent," appears on page 43.

Midge Goldberg is the editor of the anthology *Outer Space: 100 Poems*, published in 2022 by Cambridge University Press. Her third collection of poetry, *To Be Opened after My Death* (Kelsay Books), was published in 2021. She received the Richard Wilbur Award for her collection *Snowman's Code* and was the recipient of the Howard Nemerov Sonnet Award. Goldberg has also written a children's book, *My Best Ever Grandpa*. She lives in New Hampshire. Her poem, "Argument of Periapsis," appears on page 57.

Plough's 2024 poetry competition is now open. The winner receives $2000, and two finalists receive $250. All three will be published in *Plough*. Submit your new poems at plough.com/poetryaward. ✈

Feasting at Teatime

At Madonna House, taking a break is just as important as work.

Jeremiah Barker

A shrill locomotive bell, obtained decades ago from the Pennsylvania Railroad and mounted on the peak of the dishwashing porch, rings each day at 3:25 p.m. at Madonna House apostolate in Combermere, Ontario. Dozens of community members and guests stop their work, put down their tools, and get together for a cup of tea and a slice of bread with cheese, maybe an apple, and, on a lucky day, cracklings (bits of the kitchen's leftover fats and skins crisped in a frying pan). We'll sit and chat for about twenty minutes. We also have a teatime at 10:30 a.m. and another in the evening most nights of the week. It's an odd practice. Many guests wonder what this teatime business is all about. How much tea can a person drink? At Bruderhof communities, which share this practice, I hear copious amounts of coffee are consumed. At Madonna House we often serve coffee at morning tea breaks but stick with tea in the afternoons.

Our community's founder, Catherine Doherty, was a big believer in the restoration of all things in Christ (Eph. 1:10). For Catherine, a large part of what she saw as standing in need of restoration was the human capacity for simply *being*, and being *together*. This is why she was so insistent that in the midst of our work – which can indeed be holy in and of itself – we also take breaks. Breaks remind us what the work is for: work is for humanity; humanity is not for work. That is to say, as Pope Leo XIII explained in *Rerum novarum*, humanity

is the end of work and not merely a means for its accomplishment. Humanity is not to be thought of as mere capital along with the other things that play a role in the process of production, or of amassing wealth. The goal of work is the well-being of humanity.

At Madonna House, the constant back-and-forth between the call to work and the call to refrain from work is an on-the-ground, nitty-gritty reminder of the tension between the importance and dignity of work on the one hand, and the need to keep work in its proper place on the other. We stop for teatime. We stop for daily Mass. We stop for meals. We stop for the Lord's Day. We stop for major feasts.

When I was a guest at Madonna House, I asked why there is such a high ratio of staff assigned to the main center in rural Ontario compared to the small field houses scattered across the globe. Susanne Stubbs, one of the directors at the time, replied: "Here in Combermere, we're all about feasting. We put a lot of energy into preparing for Christmas and for Easter. And to put on a good feast, you need a lot of people."

By feasting Susanne didn't simply mean putting on a fancy meal and eating a lot of food – though that can be an aspect of Christian feasting, and it is at Combermere. The feast is an external expression of a deeper mystery. "Where would you like us to prepare the feast?" the disciples asked our Lord prior to the Passover (Luke 22:7–13). And, speaking of the ongoing celebration of the Lord's Supper, Paul declares, "Christ our Passover is sacrificed for us. Therefore, let us keep the feast" (1 Cor. 5:7–8).

The practice of Christian feasting isn't contingent upon having fancy food, or having a lot of food, or even having food at all. Susanne's identification of the Christian feasting that sees the birth of Christ at Christmas and his death and resurrection at Easter as the center of our communal life points to a truth at the center of Christian life in general. "What is all this work for?" I began asking myself as I fixed leaky pipes or turned compost. The answer: We're doing all this work so that we can celebrate – together, and with whoever comes our way – the feast of Christ's birth and the feast of Christ's resurrection.

"Where would you like us to prepare the feast for you?" This question became my daily prayer to Christ as I began the day, performing whatever tasks I was asked to do as a guest, and later as a community member. At Madonna House we celebrate Mass every evening in our little Island Chapel in the woods. So, in addition to looking ahead to Christmas and Easter throughout the year, as we perform the tasks of raising food, maintaining our living space, or harvesting firewood to heat our buildings, we look ahead to celebrating the birth, death, and resurrection of Christ in this daily celebration of the Lord's Supper. The gifts of bread and wine – the fruits of the earth and the work of our hands, as the liturgy puts it – we offer to God the Father, who has generously bestowed all these gifts upon us.

And really, each of our meals and, yes, each of our teatimes is an opportunity to participate in fellowship with the newborn and risen Christ in our midst, and in fellowship with one another united in him. Each day's labor, then, is preparation for the feast of Easter and the feast of Christmas that lie months, weeks, or days ahead. And just as much, each day's labor is preparation for that day's opportunities to celebrate.

So that's what the work is all about at Madonna House. That's why all these people are living together, receiving guests throughout the year, and working hard to keep the woodstoves fueled, the gardens weeded, and the animals fed. And that's what that harsh bell ringing at 3:25 each day is all about. Fundamentally, it's a call to keep the feast. We don't eat so that we can work; we work so that we can eat. We work for the feast, and the feast is for humanity's restoration and salvation. Each Christmas, each Easter, each Mass, each meal, each teatime, we celebrate Christ's birth into our midst, his resurrection from death, and the feast that is humanity's ultimate destination. ⤳

Jeremiah Barker is a lay member of the Madonna House apostolate in Combermere, Canada.

Jacopo Bassano, *Lazarus and the Rich Man*, oil on canvas, ca. 1550

The
Other Side
of the
Needle's Eye

What is money for?

PETER MOMMSEN

O NE NIGHT IN ROME around AD 404, the fabulously rich twenty-year-old heiress Melania and her twenty-four-year-old husband, Pinianus, both had the same dream. "We saw ourselves, both of us, passing through a very narrow place in a wall," Melania would later recount. "We were totally discomposed in the narrowness, so that all that remained was to give up our souls. When we came through that pain with great suffering . . . we found abundant great relief and ineffable joy. God manifested this to us, comforting our faintness of spirit, so that we might be brave concerning the future repose that we would receive after such suffering."

The "suffering" that confronted the young couple arose from their families' bitter opposition to their wish to renounce their entire fortune. Both had grown up in old-money clans with imperial connections. Their parents were Christians of varying degrees of devoutness who at the same time enjoyed living the good life as Roman aristocrats. Up until then, Pinianus and Melania had done the same (despite her longstanding misgivings). They belonged to the billionaire class of their day, owning a palace on the Caelian Hill

---

In seeking to sell off their estates outside the city, the couple freed eight thousand resident slaves.

---

and estates dotted across the Roman world from North Africa to Britain. Pinianus alone reportedly had a disposable income of 120,000 gold *solidi* per year (equivalent to 1,666 pounds or the yearly pay of 30,000 workmen).

Yet now the young couple, stirred by the recent losses of their infant son and daughter, was finding the clash between their faith and their wealth unbearable. "Sell all that you have and distribute to the poor," Jesus had told a rich young ruler who came asking how to obtain eternal life, "and you will have treasure in heaven; and come follow me" (Luke 18:18–23). Pinianus and Melania wanted to do just that. Jesus had added that it was as difficult for the rich to enter the kingdom of heaven as for a camel to pass through the eye of a needle. These words may have helped the couple make sense of their dream, the historian Peter Brown has suggested: the painfully tight cleft through which they passed into bliss was the needle's agonizing eye.

It's likely the two were also thinking of another Gospel passage that loomed large in Christian writings from that time: the parable of Dives and Lazarus. In this parable, a rich man feasts daily in luxury while the poor man Lazarus lies at his gate, covered in sores and waiting for scraps to fall from the banquet table (Luke 16). When both men die, the angels bring Lazarus to blessedness, but the rich man finds himself in the fires of hell. He begs from the flames for a drink of water, but the patriarch Abraham demurs: "Son, remember that you in your lifetime received good things, and Lazarus in like manner received evil things; but now he is comforted here, and you are in anguish." For Pinianus and Melania, this story would have struck close to home.

They found that divesting themselves of their fortune was no simple undertaking. Apart from the obstacles thrown up by their families and social circle, they faced a failed ploy by the Roman Senate to preemptively confiscate their property, while also having to fend off the schemes of opportunists. Some of their first initiatives backfired. In seeking to sell off their estates outside the city, the couple freed eight thousand resident slaves. But many other slaves revolted, refused manumission, and demanded to remain on the family lands, where they could count on food and lodging (apparently they successfully negotiated their own sale at a cut rate to Melania's brother).

Persevering, the couple found it would take years to sell the estates farther afield in Mauretania, Numidia, Gaul, Aquitaine, and Spain, some of them the size of small towns, encompassing not just farm operations but also metalworking businesses. Qualified buyers for such properties were few, even though Pinianus and Melania often took promissory notes instead of payment. The palace in Rome went unsold because none of the city's other well-heeled families had enough liquidity to pay for it. It fell into disrepair before being burned during Alaric's sack of the city a few years later.

There were moments when Melania and her husband felt the pang of renunciation, she would later tell her biographer, Gerontius. For her, one flash of regret came from recalling the colored-marble outdoor baths at one of their Italian villas, bordered by the sea on one side and a forest full of game on the other – you could watch the deer and wild boar while you bathed. For Pinianus, it was giving up his silk shirts for coarse secondhand clothes. But they didn't look back. In Gerontius' words, they had been "wounded by the divine love."

As the property sales went through, another challenge intensified: how to give away the money. Lacking a late-antique version of GiveWell, they donated somewhat at random. "Immediately they began, with zeal, to distribute" their movable goods, Gerontius writes, authorizing agents to speed up the process. "They sent money to different regions, through one man 40,000 coins, through another 30,000, by another 20,000, and through another 10,000, distributing the rest as the Lord helped them to do." They contributed 3000 coins to ransom a group of captives from pirates; paid to free children from prisons; offered stipends to young men if they swore to follow Christian disciplines; and gave 500 gold pieces to the hermit Dorotheus. Melania's wardrobe and jewelry went to churches as altar decorations. They donated the Mediterranean islands they owned to "holy men." Over time, much of their giving went to building and endowing churches and monasteries across the empire, including large donations to the diocese of the great theologian Augustine of Hippo.

From the start, they didn't just give to the poor, but also lived with them. For the first few years, they continued to stay in a spacious villa outside Rome. It soon became a thronging Christian commune that was home to thirty families and fifty single women (many of them apparently their former slaves), also offering hospitality to travelers. After five years, as the invading Goths approached the city, the couple moved to North Africa and continued their communal pattern of living there, before visiting the Christian communities in Egypt and finally moving to the Holy Land. Arriving in Jerusalem, they were enrolled

in the list of the city's poor. Pinianus became a familiar character around town, known for his only garment, a robe made of woven straw.

They stayed in Jerusalem for the rest of their lives, eventually founding several monasteries on the Mount of Olives. Pinianus died after fifteen years there; Melania survived him by seven years. When her last illness struck around Christmas 439, she was a simple nun, having earlier quashed her sisters' attempts to make her the convent's

superior. Gerontius, an eyewitness, reports that she died surrounded by her community, "tranquilly and placidly in gladness and rejoicing": a fulfillment perhaps of her dream from years before, which had promised her "ineffable joy" on the other side of the needle's eye. Her biographer adds that the only piece of linen she owned at her death was the sheet used to shroud her.

PINIANUS AND MELANIA'S STORY can sound like a colorful oddity without much modern relevance – a historical footnote from an age known for the kind of ascetic heroics that few today would imitate. But even from a secular point of view their life choices make a certain sense. Their decision to get rid of their wealth proved to be, as the newish field of study called happiness research would say, an effective investment in their wellbeing: they exchanged financial wealth for richness of relationships.

Saint Melania the Younger, miniature from the Menologion of Basil II, AD 985.

"Happiness is love. Full stop," concluded the psychiatrist George Vaillant in a 2012 interview with the *Atlantic*, summing up the results of Harvard's Grant Study, the lengthiest longitudinal research ever conducted into what makes for "successful living." This widely publicized study,

---

Today's plague of valuing money over relationships and happiness seems to have a longer backstory, one in which Christianity isn't entirely innocent.

---

launched in 1937, tracked the life paths of 268 Harvard students, among them the future US president John F. Kennedy. (It was later expanded to include the students' spouses and descendants.) The selected undergraduates were evaluated with a battery of medical and psychological tests, then tracked over the next seventy-five years with periodic questionnaires that asked about their social, professional, and family lives. Vaillant served as the study's principal investigator for more than thirty years and wrote three books about its findings.

According to Vaillant, several factors emerged from the study as key for overall life satisfaction, many of them unsurprising: having a good marriage, keeping a normal weight, avoiding smoking and alcoholism. Conspicuously, getting or staying rich was not among these key factors. Instead, reports the *Atlantic*:

> The factor Vaillant returns to most insistently is the powerful correlation between the warmth of your relationships and your health and happiness in old age. After [he first published this claim], critics questioned the strength of this correlation. Vaillant revisited the data he had been studying since the 1960s for his book, an experience that

further convinced him that what matters most in life are relationships.

If Vaillant's analysis is right, the old adage is demonstrably true: money can't buy you happiness. Love can.

IT'S A RESEARCH RESULT that ever fewer people are taking to heart. That, at least, seems to be the takeaway from a survey on American values by the *Wall Street Journal* and NORC at the University of Chicago that was released in March 2023. The poll collected the responses of more than one thousand US adults on the values they considered very important and compared their answers to a similar survey in 1998. Over that twenty-five-year span, the share of "very important" responses for several survey questions dropped precipitously: "community involvement" fell from 47 percent to 27 percent, "having children" from 59 to 30 percent, "patriotism" from 70 to 38 percent, and "religion" from 62 to 39 percent. (Viewing such results side by side with Vaillant's research, it's striking that the four declining values are all ones that, if acted on, seem likely to encourage the building of relationships.) In contrast, the share of respondents who viewed money as very important rose, from 31 percent to 43 percent, beating out all the other four values.

What explains these shifts? Here's at least the germ of a theory: Traditional religious teachings tend to subvert or at least relativize the importance of money. So when religion's influence declines, the share of those who prioritize wealth goes up. More speculatively, perhaps a loss of religious faith spills over into a loss of other kinds of faith as well – for example, in one's country, local community, and family future – thus explaining the decline in the other values as well. In any case, one prediction seems safe to make, bearing in mind Vaillant's findings about what makes for a happy life: the erosion of commitment to religion, patriotism, community involvement, and childbearing will tend to reduce the number and quality of relationships, to literally depressing effect. And that prediction matches what's actually happening all too well: according to other studies examining the decades also covered by the *WSJ-NORC* survey, the number of Americans who say they feel isolated has risen sharply, so that one in two report suffering from loneliness. As transcendent values lose their sway, money-chasing goes up, while happiness goes down.

Such an explanation may well be true as far as it goes. But in assigning all blame to the current state of our culture – a culture that, despite post-Christian drift, is still the product of a Christian heritage – it lets Christianity off the hook too easily. Is it plausible that the problem stems exclusively from twenty-first century secularization? Already two centuries ago, Tocqueville remarked on Americans' avidity for material gain, which, in his account, went side by side with a penchant for religiosity. As Eugene McCarraher describes in fascinating detail in *The Enchantments of Mammon,* parallel patterns have played out in European Christianity's relationship to wealth since the rise of capitalism. Today's plague of valuing money over relationships and happiness seems to have a longer backstory, one in which the forms of Christianity we moderns have inherited aren't entirely innocent.

Consider the question: Over the past couple of hundred years, has the bulk of Christian preaching on wealth heard in Western churches – whether mainline Protestant, evangelical, or Catholic – been of the kind apt to spur new Pinianuses and Melanias to forsake their possessions? In their day, it must be borne in mind, they were outliers only in the size of the fortune they abandoned. As Peter Brown documents in his 2011 book *Through the Eye of a Needle* (on which this essay draws), they were just two out of a multitude of lesser-known believers in the first centuries who made similar choices. In early Christianity, the idea of renouncing possessions was routine teaching, as one moral challenge among many in a young religion unafraid to make life-changing demands. In light of the Bible's strictures on wealth, the prominence of this theme in sermons preached from ancient pulpits isn't surprising. What needs explaining rather is later Christianity's relative silence, accompanied by its long détente with what Max Weber called "the spirit of capitalism" and Jesus called Mammon.

THE NEW TESTAMENT WRITINGS have now been sacred scripture for eighteen centuries, which can give them an otherworldly aura. As a result, it's easy to lose sight of just how economically radical they are. Many Christian readers tend to approach them not freshly but with the voices of later theologians whispering in their heads, offering reassurances that the words about money don't really mean what they say. So it's worth reminding ourselves just how often and insistently the New Testament hammers home its anti-wealth message.

Notoriously, the sayings of Jesus himself include some of the strongest language. He urges unstinting giving to anyone who asks (Matt. 5:42), forbids storing up wealth (6:19), discourages caring for the next day's food and clothing (6:31), and warns that to serve both God and money is impossible (6:24). He pronounces blessings on the poor and woes on the wealthy (Luke 6:20–26). His counsel to the rich young ruler to "sell all" is thus of a piece with a broader agenda, which draws on the Hebrew prophets. Although it's often noted that in this particular case Jesus' call to total renunciation applies to just one individual, in Luke's Gospel he addresses almost identical words to all his disciples (he uses second-person-plural verb forms): "Sell your possessions, and give alms . . . and you shall have treasure in heaven" (12:33–34). Two chapters later, he doubles down with an even more categorical statement: "None of you can become my disciple if you do not give up all your possessions" (14:33).

How were his followers to put such teachings into practice? Luke suggests the answer in the sequel to his Gospel, the Book of Acts, when he describes the founding of the first church in Jerusalem after Pentecost. Here, at the very moment of the Christian movement's birth, common ownership of wealth figures as an original mark of the church:

> All who believed were together and had all things in common; and they sold their possessions and goods and distributed them to all, as any had need. (2:44–45)

> Now the company of those who believed were of one heart and soul, and no one said that any of the things which he possessed was his own, but they had everything in common. . . . There was not a needy person among them, for as many as were possessors of lands or houses sold them, and brought the proceeds of what was sold and laid it at the apostles' feet; and distribution was made to each as any had need. (4:32–35)

As the theologian David Bentley Hart sums up: "Simply said, the earliest Christians were communists . . . not as an accident of history but as an

---

In time the early church's economic radicalism, though never forgotten, did come to be politely bracketed.

---

imperative of the faith." This was a communism arising voluntarily from mutual love, not from state-enforced conformity. Even for believers, it's presented as an exemplary model, not a legalistic rule. All the same, this "communism" is hardly just a spiritualized ideal, but rather a practical economic reality. The apostle Paul strikes similar notes in his repeated exhortations to the Gentile churches to practice *koinonia* – the generous sharing, including economic sharing, that for Paul is central to the Christian way (2 Cor. 8:13–15).

This anti-wealth message didn't disappear from Christianity after the faith was legalized by Constantine. On the contrary, as Charles Avila shows in his 1983 study *Ownership: Early Christian Teaching,* bishops of the fourth and fifth centuries – notably Clement of Alexandria, Ambrose of Milan, John Chrysostom, Basil of Caesarea, and Augustine of Hippo – preached fiercely and often on these very scriptural passages. The church fathers went on to root the New Testament's teachings in nature itself. As Ambrose put it:

> Nature has brought forth all things for all in common. Thus God has created everything in such a way that all things be possessed in common. Nature therefore is the mother of common right, usurpation of private right.

The Milanese bishop seems to have anticipated by fifteen hundred years Proudhon's maxim, "Private property is theft."

All this helps explain why in Pinianus and Melania's day, there had been no "Constantinian shift" on wealth, no abrupt relaxation of primitive rigor. (By contrast, in those same years the church jettisoned another of its once-widely-held convictions – that Christians may not kill – rather more rapidly and thoroughly.) Long after Christianity had become a majority faith, as McCarraher observes, "a barely repressed desire for communism . . . lurked as the political unconscious of medieval Christendom."

Even so, with the passage of time the church's economic radicalism, though never forgotten, did come to be politely bracketed. The voluntary communism of the early church survived in muffled form in Thomas Aquinas' doctrine of the universal destination of goods, the principle that ownership is not absolute but should serve the common weal. Yet at the same time, Aquinas regarded private property as a right derived from human nature, something that Ambrose and Augustine had explicitly denied. The dissonance persists within modern Catholic social teaching. Its great nineteenth-century architect, Pope Leo XIII, on the one hand retrieved the economic teachings of the church fathers, insisting that their unanimous interpretation of scripture has "supreme authority." On the other hand, following Aquinas, he also continued to teach the natural goodness of private ownership. This continues to be a source of perplexity to Catholic theologians hoping to discern a unified tradition.

The roots of this tension go back at least partly to Augustine, though he could hardly have foreseen how his words would contribute to later developments. He still strongly affirmed community of goods as the Christian ideal – he himself had renounced all his wealth, and had founded a community whose rule invoked the Book of Acts, mandating, "Do not call anything your own; possess everything in common." Yet his teachings on money from later life laid the groundwork for what was to come (it's a plotline Brown charts in greater detail in his book). As a bishop serving a growing number of rich believers, and in reaction to the self-righteous legalism he associated with various heresies, he came to regard wealth not as wrong in itself, but wrong only through misuse: "Get rid of pride, and riches will do no harm." He assured rich congregants that they could retain their wealth – not wholly innocently, since private property remained a mark of the Fall, but redeemably if they gave generous alms.

Augustine could make this move in two steps. First, he hardened a division that Ambrose had earlier made much more cautiously, distinguishing between teachings he considered binding on all Christians – the Ten Commandments, for example – and what came to be known as "counsels of perfection" applicable only to those with a special calling. Into the latter category he grouped much of the Sermon of the Mount as well as Jesus' commands to renounce possessions, even though in the Gospels these sayings are addressed to the disciples generally.

Second, he defined the existing distribution of wealth as providential: one's economic lot in life was determined by God. Riches were a gift apportioned unevenly according to the mysterious divine will, just like other unequally distributed gifts such as beauty or intelligence. For the individual Christian, the task was to use such gifts not selfishly but to God's glory.

In hindsight, the long-term ramifications of this view of wealth seem unsurprising. Defining riches as providential would prove highly welcome to those who possessed them, even as Augustine's complementary insistence on self-sacrificial almsgiving would drop into the background. By the nineteenth century, much of Christianity would affirm the class divides between rich and poor as God-ordained. In the words of a stanza from Cecil Francis Alexander's 1848 hymn "All Things Bright and Beautiful":

> The rich man in his castle,
> The poor man at his gate,
> God made them, high or lowly,
> And ordered their estate.

The hymn presents a perfect inversion of Jesus' parable of Dives and Lazarus. The rich man feasts by God's will, Lazarus waits "at his gate" by God's will, and (here comes the chorus) all is bright and beautiful. But of course, the crass difference between having and lacking money is no such thing.

S IX YEARS AGO, a friend emailed me from the village of San Jose del Sur on the island of Ometepe, Nicaragua. Did I remember Igdael, the guy we'd both worked with on the big farm outside the village twenty years ago? Igdael's twelve-year-old son Miguel had just been diagnosed with brain cancer. The doctors said treatment was urgent. It would cost ten thousand US dollars, maybe more. He knew it was a crazy request, but could I help come up with the money?

As it happened, at that moment I couldn't remember Igdael. Pulling out disposable-camera snapshots from my travels after college in the late 1990s, I puzzled over which of the men in the group photos was him. Anyway, I could be pretty sure he didn't have ten thousand dollars. My former coworkers had all been subsistence farmers; Ometepe, though a place of astonishing beauty and ecological richness, is also a cash-strapped hinterland even by the standards of the Western Hemisphere's second-poorest country. When I'd been volunteering there, the workers had brought home $3.50 a day, which on the island counted as above-average pay; from my friend's periodic reports, it sounded like not much had changed since. Although in theory Nicaragua guarantees universal free healthcare (a legal relic from the Sandinista government's optimistic early years), in reality patients must pay for anything beyond the basics. Diagnostics, drugs, chemotherapy, radiation: these would require ready money, at prices not much below those in wealthier countries.

At the same time, I didn't have ten thousand dollars either, though for different reasons. As a member of a religious community who has taken a vow of voluntary poverty, I don't have dispos-able income or a bank account. I and my family live comfortably at a living standard far above

that prevailing in San Jose del Sur, but strictly in financial terms, I own and earn nothing.

What about urging others to donate? Given my lack of billionaire friends and the dollar amount, that too seemed unrealistic, especially since my pitch to potential donors would be based only on a second-hand request from someone I barely knew. Charitable foundations would want documenta-tion, a budget, follow-up. Short of traveling to Ometepe, it was hard to imagine how to provide that. In the end, I collected a few hundred bucks from friends willing to chip in and sent a Western Union transfer.

Three months later, I asked my friend how Igdael was doing. Not good, he said. No, the boy Miguel hadn't got the treatment. Yes, he had died.

A year later, I happened to be in Nicaragua again – I was meeting the organizers of a Catholic diocesan program that *Plough* supports – and went back to San Jose del Sur for the first time since the '90s. My friend invited Igdael over. As soon as we met, I realized I did know him after all. He was great company, and an expert woodsman – I now remembered how one day he had supplied all twelve of us with a lunch of armadillo, roasted whole in its shell then sliced like a watermelon. He agreed to join us the next day and guide us through a rain forest and up the nearby volcano.

After we came back down the mountain the following evening, we visited the cemetery. They'd used the Western Union money for Miguel's grave, Igdael said. He showed it to me proudly – an aboveground cinderblock box faced with ceramic tiles, one of them screen-printed with Miguel's photo. We stood there a while and took a picture to show my own son back home.

It was strange to look at the boy's smiling portrait and wonder what his last weeks had been like and if money might have saved him. For all I know, Igdael's appeal for help to a guy from New York he'd known long ago had been one of his last desperate efforts to find a way to get his son treatment. How can it be that money, an artificial fiction created on bankers' digital ledgers, can have the power of life or death?

At any rate, Augustine was wrong about the cruel disparities in wealth being providential. Money is a human invention, after all; to blame providence for human-kind's failure to distribute it according to need is to duck our own responsibility. As Tolstoy put it: "Men pray to the Almighty to relieve poverty. But poverty comes not from God's laws – it is blasphemy of the worst kind to say that. Poverty comes from man's injus-tice to his fellow man."

Standing there, Igdael and I didn't discuss might-have-beens. He thanked me again for the money for building the grave, and then it was time to go.

OUR NEXT STOP was a meeting in San Jose del Sur to talk through plans to help those in the village who were especially badly off. A group of friends had formed a grassroots organization that operated under the umbrella of the local Catholic parish, even though some participants were Pentecostals.

For several years, they'd been working together to buy school supplies for children entering the first grade who couldn't afford the required shoes and knapsack. With the priest, they'd assembled a list of elderly people with the greatest need for assistance in getting groceries and medical care. There was a plan to buy a used truck to transport food-bank items from the mainland to the island, then transport the crops from Ometepe's subsistence farmers back to the mainland to market. Igdael was collecting hand tools to start a weekly program for teenage boys – they would fix up the public areas around the village while he taught them construction skills in the process.

By North American standards, the organizers themselves were extremely low-income. I knew that several sometimes struggled to cover the cost of food for their own families and had little in the way of savings, let alone adequate medical insurance or a retirement account. Yet rather than setting aside an emergency fund for their families – something that, given their financial precarity, might seem more than justified – they had donated sizable chunks of their earnings to others with more pressing needs.

Requests for help far outstripped the funds available. Interpersonal dynamics had to be worked through. No doubt not all the plans would come to fruition. (Though the truck did: it's been making trips for the last three years.) All the same, in a very different time and place, a community of people was setting out to do some-thing not so different from what Pinianus and Melania had done: giving recklessly, and gaining treasure in heaven.

That, Christianity suggests, is what money is for. ➤

It's not just multilevel marketing.
The whole internet wants you to
commodify friendship.

Selling Friends

CLARE COFFEY

IT STARTS WITH a Facebook message, usually. The name and picture seem vaguely, but not immediately, familiar – was there a name change since high school? The message itself is both slightly generic and relentlessly chummy, implying a long-standing, easygoing friendship rather than some half-remembered high school acquaintance.

"Hey girl!" writes Jessica (I apologize to Jessicas everywhere, but must speak from lived experience). "How have you been!? I just wanted to let you know that I've launched my own business selling [Beautycounter, doTERRA, etc., etc.], and we're having a sale right now! I wanted to make sure you didn't miss out [crying-laughing face emoji]. Let me know what you want and I'll hook you up!! Or if you ever want to chat about the amazing opportunities at Beautycounter [etc.], let me know!"

When you see this message, do not panic, disconcerting as the tenor of the whole interaction is. You have not suddenly lost your ability to

Clare Coffey is a writer living in Idaho.

appropriately match social cues with reality. The snaking tendrils of the MLM-industrial complex have merely made their way to you.

"MLM" stands for multilevel marketing, a business model in which companies recruit independent contractors to buy their products wholesale and retail them to their families, friends, and contacts. In its most famous and

---

For the most successful MLM saleswoman, friendship is not the means to the sell – it is the thing being sold.

---

successful iterations, women market products to other women, as in the Tupperware parties of the '80s and '90s, or door-to-door Mary Kay sales.

The typical MLM promises earning ability to women – it's almost always women – who cannot or do not want to access the traditional labor market. It promises almost limitless rewards, with bonuses like new cars and expensive overseas vacations lavished on top sellers. And in some cases, it delivers. MLM participants have access to two streams of income: directly from sales, indirectly from recruiting new sellers and taking a percentage of their commissions – the "downline." For a lucky few, this adds up to serious cash. For many more, it means taking a loss on wholesale products purchased more in hope than foresight, and attempting to draw on increasingly strained or diminished social networks of people who are sick of hearing about it.

The most recent iteration of MLM, reconfigured for the social-media age, bears many similarities to its forebears: small, feminine-coded consumer goods are sold by women attracted to the promise of extra income on a flexible schedule. In both cases, the business model exploits the extent and complexity of women's social networks.

But since Facebook, the transposition of social networks to social media has had effects far beyond increasing the reach and speed with which the saleswoman can deliver her pitch. Now the MLM sell has been folded into a larger pattern of self-narration, self-curation, and personal branding and social media. On Facebook and Instagram, you'll probably encounter the personal pitch described above if you hang around long enough. But the first place you are likely to encounter essential-oil agitprop (or its equivalent) will be in a post celebrating the amazing transformation that participation in an MLM has effected in the poster's life. She has been "so blessed." She has been given the tools to "take control of her own life." She "owns her own business." She is "building a legacy." She is "working with an amazing, talented, supportive group of women" who "blow her mind every day." And so, beckons the siren, can you.

You've seen the posts: the ideal representative of the typical MLM is conventionally attractive and fit, but also relatable, rocking blue jeans or yoga pants, a messy bun and an all-American million-dollar smile. She has an adoring husband and a couple of kids she stays home with, all while earning her own money. The kids feature prominently in her posts, their antics, struggles, and development all providing their own major source of content to laugh at, narrate, or charmingly deprecate. Her kitchen is farmhouse chic, and she is down-to-earth enough to occasionally post about how messy it is. She is empowered without being programmatically feminist, a girlboss within the circle of traditional domesticity. She has managed to square the circle that industrial and post-industrial economies often make of women's lives, all in a reassuringly normie way. The MLM mom's basic-ness makes her a figure of endless mockery, but it is in fact part of the sell rather than a detraction. The MLM mom is aspirational in a way that feels legitimately achievable.

This presentation is accomplished in post upon post, photo upon photo, reel upon reel. The process is not accidental, not just a byproduct of the selling process moving onto social media. It represents the perfectly matched marriage of social media's tendency to produce "curated" selves for public consumption with the business structure of MLMs. Because most MLMs are closely related to pyramid schemes, sellers often make their real money not primarily from selling, but from getting other people to sell, bringing them into their downline. The most successful MLM participant is not the one who can make her products seem the most attractive. She is the one who can make *herself* seem attractive, and proximity to her desirable – the one who can make other women want to be her, or failing that, to be her friend: to join her network, to become part of this "amazing, talented, supportive group of women" who are "launching businesses" and "building legacies."

The social media-fueled MLM suggests an example of what Aristotle calls friendship of utility, in which two people are bound together by their usefulness to each other, or their common pursuit of utility. This is what the hyperingratiating sales pitch is trying to achieve, if clumsily and one-sidedly. *She* is trying to maintain a friendship with *you* in hopes that you will buy her product. But for the most successful MLM saleswoman, friendship is not the means to the sell; it is the thing being sold. The MLM influencer is a perverse variant on Aristotle's virtuous man, who is loved for his goodness. But rather than goodness, she is loved for a kind of glossy, curated, Instagrammable excellence: the *arete* of the algorithm, the *eudaimonia* of user-generated content. And it is precisely her friendship that is for sale, for the low, low price of an entry-level shipment of product you'll have to move.

I F I SEEM UNSPORTINGLY HARSH to the aspirations of a demographic that is my own, let me hasten to add that no group so clearly mimics the dynamics of MLMs as (ahem) professional and semi-professional writers. In

In fact, if you start looking, the move from straightforward friendships of utility (common to realtors, salesmen, writers, professionals of all stripes) toward a commodification of friendship itself pops up more and more. It is the engine that drives all the parasocial professions, where posters, podcasters, content creators of all kinds can make a living from creating cultural products – many of them very good – but also from managing their own clout and their audience's desire for access to it. The parasocial professions clustering around the intersection of the gym-bro and dilettante personal-finance industries may be as paradigmatically a masculine example of the phenomenon as MLMs are paradigmatically feminine. Many men must have bought obviously worthless NFTs from their preferred weightlifting-stoicism-raw egg-supplement social media personalities, not because they had any considered belief in their value, but because it was a pledge of membership in the *männerbund* of their influencer-warlord. Surely wealth, power, "legacy-building" would flow from proximity to him just as the spoils of war were once distributed among the rank and file of a steppe khanate. He is the ring-giver; the booty he provides takes the form of creatine supplements. And though you have to pay for them, they are probably on sale.

both cases, the public-facing figure is aspirational: here, a professional doing her own creative work, far away from both the genteel indignities of nine-to-five life and the private oblivion of housewifery. In both cases, the work is usually supplemental to another source of family income. And in both cases the aspirations involved are narrowly targeted to a specific demographic: basic, Joanna Gaines–loving housewives on the one hand; English majors working at nonprofits and hoping rents don't rise faster than they can pay off their student loans on the other. And in both cases, that aspiration – and the allure of proximity that comes with it – are where the real money is. The best way to make money as a writer is not to sell words. It is to sell enough words in prestigious and fashionable spaces, to cultivate enough of a persona, that you are invited to give talks and lead workshops and finally, one day, secure a post at a creative-writing program. There, you will mentor the next generation of aspiring professional writers. More for your downline.

Plenty of writers network with each other, with various degrees of prudence, generosity, affability, and craven ambition. But you have hit an elite level when proximity to your glamor, and the possibility of your friendship, is a product you can sell.

The aspirational personal branding that enables friendship to be bought and sold as a product is a natural aspect of the every-man-for-himself, attention-driven world of the side-hustle and the independent creative. But professional nine-to-fivers should be wary about feeling too smug about what's happening in the economy's digital Ringling Brothers' circus tents. There is virtually no white-collar job that remains immune to the friendship-of-utility-to-friendship-as-commodity shift, the downward spiral from imperfect to grotesque. Indeed, LinkedIn, the internet's ground zero for professional development and networking, is to salaried workers what Instagram or Twitter is to the hustlers: a medium on which to build a personal brand through incessant self-narration. To be successful on LinkedIn, it is not enough to maintain an updated résumé and a sufficiently pleasant profile picture. Nor is LinkedIn merely the online equivalent of a Rolodex, a way to organize and maintain contact with your various professional connections. You must stake out your claim to attention and followers by developing your personal voice, unique insights, uplifting content. You must post about your #Passion, your #Inspiration, your #KeysToSuccess. You must set yourself apart from the crowd by outlining The One Mistake Most Executives Don't Know They're Making. You must be sure to salute others for their career milestones. You must frame your comings and goings from one job to another as intentional steps on the road to greatness, like the MLM mom who describes each sale as #LegacyBuilding. Above all you must present a version of yourself with no aims in life, no thoughts, no frames of reference that do not ultimately bear upon Key Performance Indicators and the rewards that follow from meeting them. From a man, you must become a Thought Leader.

Professional norms have always threatened to become totalizing. They have always been a way of making a contracted job into a way of life that touches on every other part. Friendships of utility – that old analog Rolodex – were part and parcel of this. But just as MLMs' move onto social media transformed and concentrated their dynamics, the metamorphosis of the Rolodex into a social media site meant that networking became inflected with the performance-oriented proximity-worship of Silicon Valley. In Silicon Valley, founders want access to venture capitalists. Engineers want access to founders. And the rest of the workers want the prestige, the frisson, of being ensconced where things are happening, with the people who are breaking shit and building things. Successfully projecting an image of yourself as the charismatic, visionary founder – whose proximity, comradeship, *friendship* is its own reward for service – is a way to rapidly acquire big leverage and big money, as Elizabeth Holmes understood so well.

And now this is the attitude that characterizes the performance of all professionalism. It's about passion, it's about mission, it's about getting to work with such an amazing, talented, supportive team. It is not, by any means, about anything so crude as the dollars and cents you need to take home to your family as fast as you can get out of the building. For one thing, you may or may not have a family; for another, there probably is no building.

The world of the white-collar nine-to-five, the world of the creative self-employed – in any space that marries the pursuit of money to an internet connection, you will not be able to escape the MLMification of the economy. I'm in the same boat as everyone else, on Twitter every day trying to sell my clout and land a job. I have no real solutions for creeping MLMification. Or rather, on the individual level, I have several: I could get a more useful and more difficult job assembling circuit boards at the local factory. I could build a shelter in the woods and live off small game, or at least log off. One of these days, maybe I will.

But at the level beyond individual solutions, I have more of a hope than a prescription: for the internet to recede as the primary, quasi-public, third space of American life, and with it the ability and impetus to construct palatable, consumable versions of ourselves to market to others. I hope – as long as I'm hoping – for its replacement by spaces in which we can act and appear to others, where we build and work and speak, yet where nothing – least of all our friendship – is for sale. ➤

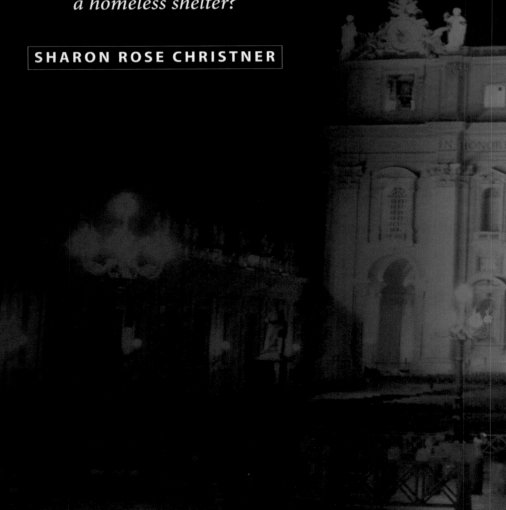

Princess
of the
Vatican

*What happens when a
Roman palazzo becomes
a homeless shelter?*

SHARON ROSE CHRISTNER

"**A**h, you are little Red Riding Hood today!" she says, seeing my red coat, and she tells me the story of the wolf and the grandmother, the great slicing open, how the girl and the old woman won back their home and their lives.

Anna and I are sitting on a low brick wall covered in cigarette ashes and tiny, resilient mosses, five steps from the border between Italy and Vatican City, in the shadow of the great travertine columns of Saint Peter's south colonnade. Every morning Anna comes out and sits on this little wall. "First, breathe. Second, smoke." Besides the cigarette, her face has quick eyes and a quicker tongue. She is tough with men and troublemakers, but soft with little ones, and forthcoming of tales with almost anyone. Most days I meet her here, and she tells me stories.

Between the columns we can see the façade of Saint Peter's and the square with its people and fountains and low wooden fences. Beyond these we can see the north colonnade and above it the Apostolic Palace where Pope Francis has chosen not to live. He stays on the side of the square where we are sitting, just around the bend and over the wall, in Casa Santa Marta, a guesthouse on the site of an ancient hostel for the poor.

The Palazzo Migliori, Anna's residence, rises behind us, looking much like its prestigious neighbors: four stories of light-yellow stucco, with a dark wood door and terraces above. Once a residence of the wealthy Migliori family, after 1930 it became the home of the Calasanziane religious order and their ministries to young single mothers. When the sisters moved out, it was proposed, given the building's beauty and desirable location, that it be converted into an upscale boutique hotel. Pope Francis directed that it be made into a homeless shelter instead.

The shelter opened in November 2019; as I sit with Anna a few months later, the place is developing a rhythm. Every evening just before seven – while others are pitching tents around the colonnade, or lying down on the front steps of shops, or wrapping themselves in blankets under the bridges of the Tiber – a little group gathers by the door of 28 Borgo Santo Spirito. Up the ramp in his chair comes Mario, always with Luigi pushing him, and like a dignitary he waves and calls *buonasera* to Marya and Lilia and all the ladies whose names he does not know; Alessandro, quieter, who actually knows all the names; a thin and grinning Ajim, who has just come from the soup kitchen on Via Dandolo and is hungry again; Anna, spinning yarns between cigarettes; Mirella, neck tilted all the way back, talking with the men and finding something to be right about. At seven, someone opens the door and they get themselves through the hallway to the chapel, slowly, because it has been a long day on the feet. They greet each other and sit quietly in the pews, looking up occasionally at the painted wood-panel ceilings or the mural of Saint George, armored and haloed, battling a dragon. The people who have been upstairs cooking come in, drying their hands on their aprons. One of them goes behind the altar and leads a prayer, reflecting on the presence of Jesus with them. The congregation shares a sign of peace, everyone finding everyone else's hand. Then, with their heavy bags, they make their way up, by stairs or elevator, to dining rooms which, with their chandeliers and brickwork archways, could be chapels themselves.

Sharon Rose Christner is a student at Harvard Divinity School. She is currently writing a book about homelessness in and around Vatican City. She has written for Prairie Schooner, Philadelphia Stories, *and the* Philadelphia Citizen.

Already good bread is on the table. Dinner is brought out in courses – olive-tomato fettuccine or creamy white bean soup, then pork mushroom stew or beef pot roast. When everyone has been served, the people who have come to cook sit and eat with the people who have come to sleep. I could call them volunteers and guests, but such a distinction misses the point. I might call them the residents, who sleep here each night, and the visitors, who sleep somewhere else. Everyone eats together, and is called by name, and afterward there are chamomile teas and baskets of fruit and much talking.

Anna tells stories, and stories of stories. If you notice her hat, a white knit cap with a Hello Kitty patch, she will tell you:

A baby gave me this! I was at the park, on the bench. The mother? She is on the phone talking, talking . . . So I talk with the girl, nine or ten years old. I tell her a story: Once there was a girl, and she learned how to knit hats, and she became very rich – just a story, like Cinderella – and she met a prince who liked her hats.

So the mother is finally done speaking, and the little girl says, "At least take my hat." I say, "How can I wear the thing of a baby? I am old!" But the mother says, "Please, she has ten of these in all the different colors. So if she offers, please take it." I never thought I would wear the hat of a baby! But now I wear it so I can tell this beautiful story.

Others bring stories too, in many languages and silences, and they bring out their cigarettes to share on the terrace. The genius Silvano brings his Rubik's Cube, clicking and whirring, and sometimes a gray-haired priest comes up the stairs bringing gifts. The first time I visited, Cardinal Konrad Krajewski, the papal almoner, brought a wide woven basket of cinnamon-sugar pastries and fancy jams. He spread them out on the counter and didn't let anyone call him Your Eminence.

Several times each week, a physician comes and speaks with everyone who will allow her, looking closely at what is hurting. Someone's ear, someone's back, everyone's throbbing feet. Often someone comes in late around this time,

The inaugural dinner of the guesthouse, run by the Community of Sant'Egidio, in Palazzo Migliori, November 2019.

if the buses of Rome have failed them. Not long ago Anna herself came up the steps at nearly ten, after everything had been put away, announcing, "I won't eat!" in great penitence. Nonsense, they said, of course you can eat. "I can eat it cold, whatever, just pasta, because I came late. It's my fault, *è colpa mia.*" No, they insisted, of course you can eat the whole meal. Anna really must, because her medication requires food, but for anyone, medication or not, the visitors will get out the fettuccine, the pork and mushrooms, the bread, tea, salt, pepper, and oil, as many times as necessary.

At length it becomes more and more like bedtime, and people say goodnight and ascend to the third and fourth floors, where thirteen bathrooms with soap and towels have been prepared for them, and sixteen bedrooms with clean sheets and blankets. In the morning there will be breakfast, and then they will leave for the day, and more visitors will come to clean. For now, for each person there is a usual spot, several accustomed roommates, a place to put their things down for a while and sleep. The visitors come and knock and say goodnight, *buona notte,* to each one by name.

SUCH AN OVERFLOWING PLACE invites questions: Why such extravagance? Why not make the place into a hotel, rake in the money, and set up a no-frills shelter in a lower-cost part of Rome? Instead of giving beautiful treatment to fifty people, should they not provide more practical lodging to a hundred?

We could wish for a world without such calculations. But if we must calculate, it depends on the goal. If we are trying to get as many people as possible indoors – when the temperature is unsurvivable – the austere one-hundred-bed place is better. This is the purpose of an emergency shelter, and it is good that we have them. But if the situation is different – if the climate is mild and many people do not want to come indoors – the goal might be to create a stable, dignified place for those who want to come.

For either kind of place, there is always the question: Will people choose to stay? Anna, and many others, have been in other shelters and decided that it would be safer, or less demeaning, to take their chances outside. Often this is a simple matter of which is more hospitable to human life. If an "efficient" shelter has an atmosphere of danger, contempt, or the bare-minimum keeping of livestock, any of us might choose the outdoors.

Once, the Gospels tell, when a woman poured perfume on Jesus' feet and washed them with her hair and tears, Judas Iscariot was suddenly concerned about efficiency. "Why wasn't this perfume sold," he objected, "and the money given to the poor? It was worth a year's wages." Jesus told him to let her be, for she had done a beautiful thing, preparing his body for burial. It turned out that Judas objected not because he cared for the poor but because as holder of the moneybag he felt entitled to keep the excess for himself.

Those of us who have charge of funds and decisions, and who have mostly had it easy, can take austerity on ourselves. But when it comes to caring for others, that is the place to be generous to excess, to give more than seems necessary.

Palazzo Migliori is not the kind of shelter where you line up each day and try to get a place. Carlo, the director, identifies people without another place to go: those especially alone, or more fragile, or without the citizenship that certain shelters require. They stay a few weeks at least. The staff help residents find stable situations – in these first few months several have found jobs and family reunion – but there is no set deadline for leaving. The mental strain of trying to find a bed each night is lifted, and there is room to come to know the others around you, even to trust them; to start to think in terms of weeks, months, years.

Now Anna has begun to think beyond the food-shower-sleep cycle to plan her own kindnesses. This morning on the little wall she is waiting to catch the bus to the hospital where her closest friend, Concetta, is sick with something like the flu. Yesterday Anna helped her onto a bus and off the bus and onto another bus to the hospital, while Concetta's breaths turned into brittle rasps. Today, she will convince the nurse to let her

into the room again, and she will sit by her friend and talk. Speaking will be difficult for Concetta, but she can still hear stories.

Some of the stories will be from books, chosen according to Concetta's mood and interest, and by the feeling of the story, which depends most of all on its ending. They have been friends for forty years, half their lives, so many of the stories will be true: wistful stories of wishing for countryside

---

Those of us who have charge of funds and decisions, and who have mostly had it easy, can take austerity on ourselves. But when it comes to caring for others, that is the place to be generous to excess, to give more than seems necessary.

---

homes, or the heroic story of Concetta trying to help Anna when she first lost her job and things began to spin downward.

Anna has only begun to speak to me about what happened then, and never in detail – the circumstances of her youth, what happened to her family, the causes of her grief – but she has told the general story. When she lost her home she stayed "in no place, any place. To sleep? No sleep. Sitting. Upright like this. It was horrible. Always where there was a camera, because I was afraid. And, in the winter, wherever it was hot. A camera for safety, and warmth to survive."

She remembers pedestrians taking wide circles to avoid coming near her, passersby steeling their faces. "Because everybody – except my friend, who is in the hospital – is afraid of poorness. They cannot afford, emotionally, to see *themselves* in that situation. So they become blind.

"You start from a normal life, then suddenly *boom*, everything is broken, even if it's not your fault." She snaps her fingers. "Just like that! You fall into a whirlpool, and you drown!

"And then? God is good. He, the *big* father, saw this little thing falling down, and he picked me out and put me here. Straight away, without any problem!" – here she becomes quieter – "Without any important reason either. Because I didn't do anything so *great*" – she spreads her arms wide – "to stay in a palace next door to the pope! Like a *princess,* oh my. So if anyone doesn't believe that miracles can happen . . ."

WHEN ANNA TELLS STORIES, the ending determines the rest. A good end, in a palace with a bed and good food and people who know her, allows her to think of her life the same way she tells a fairy tale. The story could have ended, "and little Anna lived out her days in a dimly-lit, understaffed facility." Instead, it ends: "and now I am in the place of a princess."

This place gives Anna a story that bends toward peace and rests there. Something about its over-the-top-ness: the carefully painted crests on the ceiling, the terrace overlooking Saint Peter's Square, the unnecessarily good food. The visitors who know your name and your favorites and your good and bad habits, who know you need to put that cream on your foot and will banter with you until you do it. Above all it is knowing: that this place could have been a posh hotel; that some might call its current incarnation a waste; that you are not being given the bare minimum.

When we love someone, we are not thinking of how to do so efficiently; we are thinking how to do it well. Think of new parents preparing a beautiful nursery: they may buy things the child never uses, and perhaps some of that money and effort might be better used elsewhere. But we are not surprised when loving parents put more thought and work into preparing a place than is strictly necessary.

There are certain things that we know make a good place for anyone – shelter from the cold, a quiet place to sleep, a warm stew, a clean place to wash up, art, song, softness – and we can prepare these things even before we meet the recipients. Once we meet, there begins the work of making it a good place for them in particular – for Astriche, who loves chamomile; for Lioso, who is so much more tired than hungry and just wants to *sleep*; for Ajim and his appetite; for Anna the teller of tales.

Just before Jesus was betrayed and arrested, he comforted his troubled friends with a strange promise: "I am going to prepare a place for you" – his father's house with many rooms. We think of the way someone prepares a place for us when they know us well; we can only imagine how someone prepares a place for us when they know us completely. For now, there is this quiet joy of making a place beautiful with someone in mind – of considering who they are, what they need and love and fear, and shaping the place to meet them.

It is by design that Francis lives in a guesthouse and Anna lives in a palace. One's austerity is another's luxury, and all things considered the pope still lives in more material comfort than she does. But the direction is a promising one. When we are healthy and loved, it is good and wise to be content with simple, humble things. When we are trying to love and heal someone, on the other hand, we should offer more than they could ask or imagine.

"So," Anna finishes, "the building is *fantastic.* Outside, it doesn't give so much emotion, but the inside is fantastic. If you were to tell me before that from the beginning to the end God was bringing me close to the pope, living in a wonderful place, loved by everybody – this is great. All the rest is . . ." She gestures *gone,* and leans back to look up at the many rooms. "Who could imagine?" ⤳

Clair de lune

from Claude Debussy's Suite Bergamasque
in memory of my mother

There's D-flat major at the first and last,
but in between, a haze of harmonies
yearns lightward, though the light has long since passed.

I played the notes; she heard the light. The keys
were mine to coax and animate; their sound
was hers to claim: a shimmer of heart's ease.

And while my fingers stretched and danced and found
their way through black and white, her ear would find
a prism—her own light parsed and unbound.

She had a knack for joy and was inclined
to wonder. *Clair de lune* had mesmerized
her, in a spell that left me far behind.

After my mother's death, I was surprised
I still played it so often; I suppose
the effort occupied and organized

my sorrow-scattered mind. So in the throes
of grief, I practiced, as if I'd impress
a ghost with my devotion. And in those

half-haunted hours, I mastered more, I guess,
than just the notes. I hadn't thought I'd learn
to hear what she did—but through some finesse

of time and skill and need, I now discern
the half-lit murmurings that no midnight
can mute, the moon-pale promise that can turn

unrest to peace, a star-sung appetite
for breath. At last I share my mother's light.

JEAN L. KREILING

Mark Wagner, *Duh-Dunt*, currency on panel, 2012

Enchanted
Capitalism

*Modern capitalism claims to be secular.
It's anything but.*

EUGENE McCARRAHER

Plough's Peter Mommsen speaks with Eugene McCarraher about Christianity's compromise with mammon – and the visionaries who have resisted it.

Peter Mommsen: We're living in a moment when capitalism is again being questioned around the world, and yet still seems amazingly resilient in spite of its crises. What's your view of the state of capitalism today? Are the threats to it serious?

Eugene McCarraher: I do think capitalism is seriously threatened, though that doesn't necessarily mean I think it's going to collapse next week or next month, or even in the next couple of decades. Clearly it's now a very fragile system: over the past three decades it seems to have needed constant rebooting by government money. Whether that's the tech collapse of 2000, the banking collapse in 2008, or the FTX crash just last year, the market seems to need more and more propping up.

Eugene McCarraher is professor of humanities and history at Villanova University. He is the author of The Enchantments of Mammon *(Belknap Press, 2019).*

So I do think that this is a very precarious system. I'd even say it's in a state of terminal decline. But that's going to look like languishing, rather than collapse, I think. There's a German sociologist I quote near the end of *The Enchantments of Mammon*, Wolfgang Streeck, who talks about capitalism in our time as being a kind of zombie system. It's almost dead, but thanks to all kinds of state support, the damn thing never quite dies.

So I think capitalism is probably going to continue for a while in this strange state where it's materially all-powerful but politically and ideologically vulnerable in a way it never was during the halcyon days of neoliberalism.

Capitalism, as most people think of it, apart from just being a fact of life, is frequently presented as a neutral social technology to enable maximum human flourishing. Could you walk us through the reasons why you disagree with that claim?

First of all, I don't think technology, social or otherwise, is ever neutral. And the reason I think this is that technology is made by human beings, and therefore technology always embodies some kind of human interest. So, just on the level of definition, I find the idea that technology is occupying some kind of Archimedean point of complete objectivity unpersuasive.

I guess the other thing – and something I take issue with in *The Enchantments of Mammon* – is the idea that capitalism has taken us out of poverty and misery and oppression and destitution. That's one of the arguments often made for it: that it's brought us this great material progress. And I think the story is more complicated than that.

I don't deny that we are materially better off than we were in the Middle Ages. We are, by and large, healthier; we live longer; we are better educated. I don't deny any of that. But I think a lot of the material progress that we've made is only distributed with any degree of equitability thanks to political movements. It was because we had things like labor unions and political parties that we were able to organize society in a more humane way. It's not something that capitalism does naturally at all.

Fixating on material progress evidences a failure of moral imagination. The way we evaluate the economy is asking, "How much stuff did we produce last year?" We don't ask whether any of the stuff that we produced actually contributed to human flourishing. We don't distinguish things like fruit and vegetables from cigarettes and nuclear weapons. It's all economic growth. There's no kind of moral evaluation involved.

Not to mention that we're talking about a system that requires infinite growth operating on a planet with finite resources. We're only beginning to reckon with the environmental price that we've had to pay for that.

I think we know, as a society, that all of this is bad, and yet we don't seem to be able to act any differently. I think a major reason for that is that we don't know what we want. Even though capitalism isn't ideologically invulnerable to the same degree that it was, we don't have any conception of what an alternative way of life would be. So we default to the status quo.

I'd like to talk about this word *enchantment*, which is so key in your book. Capitalism, even by its critics, is usually thought of as fundamentally secular – as disenchanted. Karl Marx, for example, said, "Capitalism drowns the most heavenly ecstasies of religious fervor in the icy water of egotistical calculation." And Max Weber famously popularized the thesis that capitalist modernity is this process of disenchantment. You take issue with this view and argue that capitalism is no less enchanted than the worldviews it supplanted. What does it mean that capitalism is enchanted – and why does that matter?

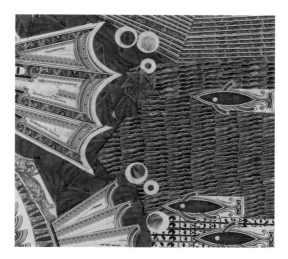

I think capitalism is fundamentally enchanted because we treat it with this sacred awe and veneration. We tell ourselves, no, we don't really revere the dollar, we don't really consider it sacred – well, in practical terms, we do. The reason we do that is because, under capitalism, money actually does become an arbiter of what's good – or even what's real.

When I get business students in my college classes, I'll say, "Look, you guys in standard economics, you have this notion called effective demand, right?" They'll say, "Yes." I say, "Effective demand says that if I'm thirsty, but I don't have any money to pay for, say, a bottle of water, my thirst, as far as the market is concerned, does not exist. Am I right?" And they'll say, "Yeah, that's true. Your thirst has no effective demand."

Now, you and I both know that I'm still thirsty even if I can't afford to quench it. But in the eyes of the market, my thirst is nonexistent. And, as I point out to my students, that economic fact is also a moral statement, an ontological assertion. The market is an ontology, a way of deciding not only what is right and wrong, but what is real and what is unreal. And that's exactly the kind of power we used to attribute to God.

In the past, humans generally believed that the metaphysical structure of the world was determined by God. In a capitalist society, money plays that role: without money, you, or at least your needs as a human being, don't exist. Right at the heart of disenchantment, we find this clearly theological dynamic. And this was noticed by none other than Karl Marx.

Marx was of two minds about disenchantment because he did say, as you quoted him from *The Communist Manifesto*, that capitalism is this secularizing, disenchanting force that reduces everything to calculation. He's also the guy who, in the very first volume of *Das Kapital*, introduces what he calls "commodity fetishism" by describing the fungible products of capitalism, what he calls "commodities," as "abounding in metaphysical subtleties and theological niceties."

He explains that in the capitalist marketplace, the value of something is determined in pecuniary terms, not whether it's useful or not, not whether it's morally or humanly good or not. It's all about what it can fetch in the marketplace. In other words, in capitalism, according to Marx, there's this process – "fetishization" – where we attribute all kinds of powers to money that it only really has because of us and the way that we act.

I think capitalism is historically unique in this regard, but lots of ancient societies were very suspicious of the power of money. Across so many

cultures, not just in the Near East where it was given the name Mammon, money is deified, and not in a good way. Mammon is the spirit of acquisition, the spirit of ruthlessness. It's a bad god.

There's a quote I love from the theologian Jacques Ellul on this. He writes: "Money is a power. This term should be understood, not in its vague meaning of force, but in the specific sense in which it is used in the New Testament. Power is something that acts by itself, is capable of moving other things, is autonomous or claims to be, is a law unto itself, and presents itself as an active agent."

Yeah. I think the really important part of that Ellul quote is about money presenting itself as being an active agent, an autonomous power. One thing that I think the Marxist tradition is very strong on – and something I think Christians especially should pay attention to – is the idea that the power of money is our own power that we have somehow deified as something external to us.

Speaking of money as a power, of course, brings us to the New Testament. There's a saying of Jesus that is familiar to all of us: "No one can serve two masters. You cannot serve both God and mammon" (Matt. 6:24). So what is mammon, and how does using this term change how we think about capitalism?

Well, mammon in the New Testament is a god, or at least a spirit – a demon. It's a demon who encourages greed, stupidity, endless dissatisfaction, all for the purposes of endless acquisition. The reason I think it's important to talk about mammon as a spiritual force, and the reason I think that's important for our understanding of capitalism, is that we usually understand capitalism strictly as a political economy.

Whether we're Marxists or liberals or conservatives we usually think about it in terms of a certain configuration of markets, and property, and the state. Yet it seems to me that capitalism is also, I think, a kind of moral imagination, and a certain form of spiritual formation. That's what I'm getting at when I use the term "mammon": that capitalism remains "enchanted," it retains this spiritual, moral dimension. We don't usually think of capitalism as a spiritual force, of course, but I think that's what it is.

And I think recognizing that helps us to see what the system really is, beneath the surface. So in my book I argue that we should start understanding advertising as a form of iconography, for example: images that visibly disclose an invisible reality. I think that this is actually one of the best ways to try to explain what's going on in advertising, because you're not just selling goods with advertising, you're inviting viewers to enter a whole moral universe.

Which is exactly what the stained glass windows of saints in Chartres Cathedral are doing. The rose window and the highway billboard both have a set of values embedded within them: a certain conception of what's right and what's wrong. And those values are a kind of spiritual formation, directing your soul toward a particular end, a particular eschatology.

In Chartres, that eschatological vision is heaven, the kingdom of God, the beloved community, whatever you want to call it. Within advertising's symbolic universe, under capitalism, your spiritual formation has the particular end of accumulation, how to make the most money possible. Heaven is a fat bank account.

Throughout Christian history believers have responded to Jesus' warning about mammon in different ways. Acts 2 and 4 paint a picture of the first believers holding all things in common, sharing according to their ability, receiving according to their need. What is the importance of that voluntary communism and what distinctions should we make between it and the political communism of the twentieth century?

What this depiction demonstrates is that the early Christians were communists with a small c. I cannot reiterate that enough.

For centuries Christians have found all kinds of laughable exegetical strategies to try to make the text not say what it clearly does say: that the early church held their goods in common, and that they distributed those goods according to need. Especially during the Cold War, there was an obsession with trying to make this text say something entirely different from what it actually says.

And the reason why there was that obsession is because it demonstrates that communism is the political unconscious of Christianity, right? Small-c communism – it's not as though the early Christians had some kind of program for changing society. So that's one distinction.

One of the other really key differences between the two communisms is that Marxism, in a sense, shares a worldview with capitalism. Capitalists are always talking about growth, technological innovation, the constant production of material abundance. And it's very clear when you read *Das Kapital* that Marx has the same basic worldview. Marx views technological development and material abundance as goods in themselves, regardless of any other end. That's not what the early Christians thought at all. So that to me is, I think, the defining difference between the two forms of communism.

Even long after the Book of Acts, Christians remain pretty nervous about money. So it's striking how big a role Christianity ended up playing in the rise of capitalism. How did Christianity come to make peace with mammon?

I think it's part of a much longer story of compromise. The peace that was struck with mammon was, in a sense, modeled on the peace struck with Caesar in what's sometimes called the Constantinian Bargain. The Constantinian Bargain was that if you swear your allegiance to the structures of imperial Rome, we'll leave you guys – you guys being the Christian church – alone. We'll tolerate you guys, we'll let you guys preach, we'll let you perform your liturgies.

As soon as you make that kind of bargain with Caesar and, if we want to use another god, with Mars, the god of the military and of war, there's a sense in which peace with mammon is inevitable. If you're coming to some kind of understanding with the powers that be I think it's part of the deal.

Yet there is this counter-tradition within church history – a stream of people throughout who did not go along with this, who were critics of compromise, who harked back to those original "communist seeds" of Christianity and tried to bring them to life.

Yeah, the name I give to this counter-tradition is capital-R Romanticism. It includes Christians across the theological spectrum, from the mainstream down to the heterodox, like William Blake. And it includes non-Christians, both religious and non-religious, like John Ruskin, who retain a kind of post-Christian worldview.

Basically, I think Romantics are the heirs to the medieval sacramental imagination. That imagination said: God is everywhere, God suffuses the natural world, the material world. And that worldview was sacramental in that it perceives the divine as a constitutive part of the architecture of the world. You can see this in Blake's famous line about seeing the heavens in a wildflower, or Wordsworth writing about his sense of the sublime suffusing all things.

Some people see Romanticism as a discrete literary and artistic movement, starting in the eighteenth and nineteenth centuries, and ending with World War I at the very latest. I think Romanticism is actually a distinctive feature of modernity itself, from the English Civil War, Gerrard Winstanley, and the Diggers right up to the 1970s with figures like Kenneth Rexroth, Thomas Merton, Dorothy Day, and to the present day with figures like Pope Francis – who I think in many ways belongs in that Romantic lineage.

And as you can guess from that list, the Romantics are, for me, a very big tent. But the tent isn't so big that the label itself is meaningless. They share some general characteristics. So many of the Romantic figures in my book see labor as properly artisanal rather than mechanical, the act of labor itself as a kind of poetry in action. Often they're in favor of direct workers' control over production; a recurring theme is that they believe technology should be on a more human scale. Many are anarchists or political radicals. Even when they accept some version of private property rights, they also see property as always in some sense communal. And because they don't see nature solely in terms of how useful it can be to human beings, they're often far more ecologically sensitive than their peers.

How do you hope people persuaded that there is an alternative to capitalism will live their lives differently? One of your book's conclusions is that there is a need to begin from "a realized eschatology," a way of "living the new world in the wreckage of the old." What would that look like in practice?

This is the question that I always try to avoid because it's where I go from being a historian, writing about the past, to some kind of prophet making predictions about our political future. I think in many ways the fundamental practice is to be a good Christian. Being loving and charitable and merciful in one's own life. As for the exact political shakeout of that practice, I'm not entirely clear myself on what that is. I think it means supporting a revitalized labor movement, because if we're going to get a handle on things like AI or the ecological crisis, then we have to be rooted in workplace struggles over the design and the deployment of technology.

What I think also needs to be done is that we've got to have activism within the churches: Protestant, Catholic, Orthodox, the whole American church establishment. We all are guilty. We've all chosen Mammon over God. We've allowed ourselves to be spiritually formed by capitalism, shaped by the logic of the markets. But we're also all capable of realizing a different eschatology, living for a different end, seeking the kingdom of God. We need to learn how to be Christians. ➤

This interview from March 20, 2023, has been edited for clarity and length. To listen to a longer audio version, visit *plough.com/mccarraherinterview*.

Louis Comfort Tiffany, *Pumpkin and Beets window*, stained glass, 1900.

Advent

A pumpkin vine is far from where its roots
first sprang into the earth. It seeks the sun,
proceeding south as fast as it can run.
With luck, it adventitiously re-roots
itself when it can find the ground, re-routes
itself in random zigzags to outrun
the pestilence, the drooping of the sun,
that stanch the flow from soon-abandoned roots.
It seems as though it never has to die
as long as it continues on its way
away from rots that chase it from its roots,
adventuring beneath renewing skies,
discarding golden blossoms day by day—
until it finds that it's arrived, and fruits.

MATTHEW KING

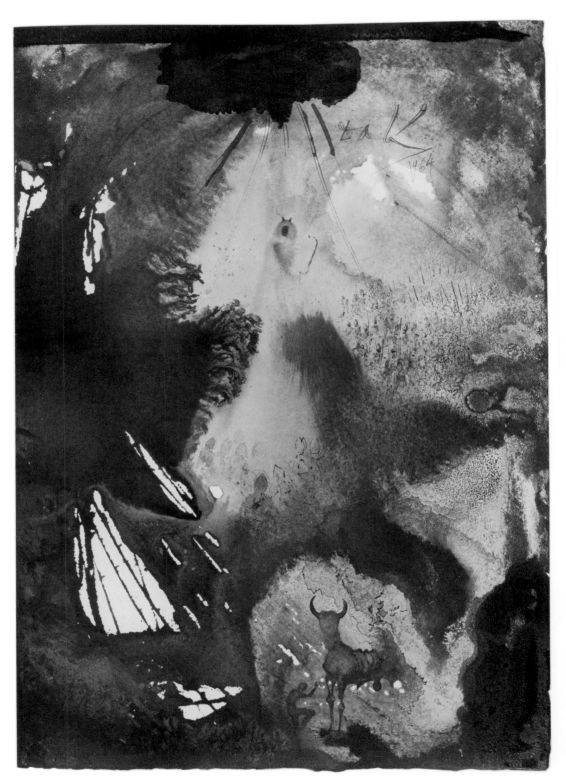

Salvador Dalí, *I Am The Lord Your God*, lithograph, 1964

THE
RELIGION OF
Mammon

Money and God are enemies.
We must choose one or the other.

EBERHARD ARNOLD

Eberhard Arnold, **Plough's** *founding editor, wrote the following essay in 1923 in the wake of World War II and the Bolshevik Revolution. It has been abridged and edited for clarity.*

MANY PEOPLE ASSUME that every form of religiosity belongs together in the same category: *religion*, which stands in contrast to everything nonreligious and secular. This way of dividing up social and personal life is misleading. To be sure, there is a dividing line to be drawn, but it cuts right across the categories of religious and secular. It is the line Jesus drew when he declared: "You cannot serve God and Mammon" (Matt. 6:24).

Early Christianity keenly recognized that the religiosity of the present world epoch is hostile to God. The new faith's first witnesses brought the message of God's "totally other" kingdom (to use Karl Barth's phrase), of what Nietzsche called the "transvaluation of all values." The Christians bore witness to this message of the totally different

Eberhard Arnold (1883–1935), a German theologian, was cofounder of the Bruderhof. The full version of this essay appears in his book Salt and Light: Living the Sermon on the Mount, *forthcoming in a new edition in October 2023 (Plough).*

order to come, calling it the message wrapped in mystery, concealed from those who are lost, whose thoughts have been blinded by the god of this world (2 Cor. 4:4).

Opposed to the God whose arrival is imminent – the God who will establish the kingdom of Jesus Christ with its justice, unity, and love, the God of the beginning and the end – stands an interim god, the god of this world epoch. This god is the spirit of this world, the "earth spirit" familiar to us from modern literature.[1] This god

---

Why do these facts remain hidden from us? It is because we ourselves are also under the dominion of the god Mammon, and so lack the strength to rebel against it.

---

of greed, of murderous possessiveness, of grasping and holding, is the spirit of this world. The first witnesses testified that we have not received the spirit of this world, but the Spirit that searches the depths of God, the Spirit that nobody can know without being known by him (1 Cor. 2:10–12).

No one can serve two masters; you cannot serve God and Mammon. Jesus defined with utmost sharpness the nature of Mammon as a spirit, unmasking the true nature of the religiosity of the propertied classes. He showed how this religiosity worships a spirit of death.

Jesus taught that Satan, the leader of unclean spirits, is also "the murderer from the beginning" (John 8:44). Mammon kills; its very nature is murder. It is through the spirit of Mammon that wars have broken out and impurity has become an object of commerce. Nor does it only kill through war. Every day that drives hungry children and the unemployed into villages seeking food, only

to be chased out again by farmers with their dogs, shows us Mammon's murderous nature. We have become used to the reality that numberless people are being crushed to death through our affluence, just as one might grab a bug and squash it; we have ceased to give a thought to those who are destroyed because of us. Today even the blindest must see how Mammon's development means the incessant murder of hundreds and thousands.

In the form of large-scale capitalism, Mammon achieves its dominance through its lying power. During the war, we learned how lying and killing belong together as twins, since one cannot wage war without a basic inner mendacity. In the same way, a capitalistic society can only be maintained by large-scale deception, a denial that any other way of living is possible.

But we are a long way from revolting against this lie. *Rich and poor must be* – this is the common thinking in pious circles, and even among the working classes. People say things like: "When a man who manages thousands of millions of gold marks is able to give work and a livelihood to a large number of people, we have to accept the situation and be glad that such an energetic personality exists." But this view completely ignores the fact that it is impossible to amass such a degree of wealth – which at the same time means power – without cheating, depriving, hurting, and even killing one's fellow human beings along the way. It fails to see that since capital is concentrated in so few hands, the decision of one man can steer hundreds of thousands to ruin through unemployment, as is happening today.

WHY DO THESE FACTS remain hidden from us? How is it possible that our fellow human beings are incessantly cheated of justice and yet we remain blind to this? It is because we ourselves are also under the dominion of the god Mammon, and so lack the strength to rebel against it.

---

1. The silent film *Erdgeist* ("*Earth Spirit*") was released in the same year Arnold was writing, based on Frank Wedekind's play of the same title.

Mammon is money ruling over people, over human life itself, which is made dependent on monetary income and financial circumstances. So long as we rely on money for our own existence and security, we will not be in a position to pull the lever that lifts Mammon's enslaving rule off its hinges. Even so, we can at least recognize the enmity that exists between money and God.

God or Mammon; spirit or money. Spirit is the deep relationship between living things, the innermost connection between them. Human beings are in constant relationship with one another; no one leads an utterly isolated life. People are interrelated in groups, families, classes, and professions; in nations, states, churches, and all kinds of associations. Above and beyond these connections, they are interrelated in a much deeper way simply through being human, as members of the great, growing fellowship of humankind.

Money objectifies these relationships, changing them from spiritual to material, until it becomes the only value left. Instead of remaining merely a means of exchange, money becomes a commodity in itself. What we have then is money in its essence, money as power.

That is why money and love are mutually exclusive: money is love's opposite, just as killing people in war, commercializing the sexual defilement of bodies, or lying to the public are all love's opposites. And that is why, too, everything concerning Mammon is a question of which religion we put our trust in.

ESUS DECLARED WAR on the spirit of Mammon. He conquered this spirit of weakness by overwhelming and healing victims of sickness and decay with his power. He lived among us human beings in order to take away death's power – to destroy death, the devil's work (1 John 3:8). The spirit of life that proceeds from Christ overcomes, too, the death of the inner life, and brings fellowship among all living things; as

he exclaimed, "Now is the judgment of this world; now the prince of this world will be cast out" (John 12:31). The Spirit will convince humanity that this prince is defeated (John 16:7–11).

As soon as we side with Jesus, we must be ready to forswear Mammon, overcome it, and declare war on it. When our inner eye has opened to see his light, our eye will stop responding to Mammon's will (Matt. 6:22–23). We will no longer be able to amass wealth when our hearts are set on the new future, when we have the hope that God will establish a new kingdom. Then we will strive only for this one thing and will turn our backs on everything else. We will live for the future that is humanity's freedom, humanity's unity, and humanity's peace. Then we will be able to fulfill Jesus' teaching to "make friends for yourselves through unjust Mammon" (Luke 16:9) by giving Mammon away and gaining love in doing so.

Numerous episodes from Jesus' life illustrate what living free of Mammon looks like. When a rich, pure-minded young man who was not

When someone was needed to manage the disciples' common purse on the long journey, Judas was asked to be the keeper: Judas, who Jesus knew would become the betrayer (John 12:6). The murderer from the beginning was exposed in the very company of Jesus' disciples. Judas ended where murder must end. He disclosed the secret that Jesus knew he was the Messiah King of the completely different order. Jesus stood his ground when questioned by the political and religious authorities: "Are you the Messiah, the Son of the Highest?" He answered, "I am; you will see the Son of Man seated at the right hand of Power, and coming on the clouds of heaven to establish his kingdom" (Mark 14:61–62). They put him to death on the basis of this revolutionary confession. With Jesus eliminated, the spirit-born community he led was seemingly destroyed. The will of Mammon, the will of death, seemed to have triumphed in the end.

Yet through the very execution of the leader of this new order, through the grave itself, life won out. Amazingly, from this downtrodden people, the Jews, young men and women met to wait together for something completely new. They waited for the Spirit. They knew that this spirit of love, order, and freedom was the spirit of God's kingdom. And the Spirit came upon them, bringing about a church community, a fellowship of work and goods in which everything belonged to everyone and all members were active to the full extent of their varied powers and gifts (Acts 2).

aware of having done anything wrong came to Jesus, Jesus loved him at first sight and asked him whether he loved God and his neighbor. The young man thought he had done everything he needed to do. "Good," said Jesus. "If this is really the case, then what you need to do now is to make this love real. Go and sell everything, give it to the poor, and come with me" (Matt. 19:16–21).

The god Jesus met when he entered the temple, the sanctuary of Jewish religion, was not his God, but the god Mammon: cattle and cattle dealers, banks and bankers. Jesus made a whip, not to strike people in the face but to forcibly overturn the tables and show his contempt for money by throwing it on the floor. He testified that this house should belong not to Mammon but to God (Matt. 21:12–13). When a spy came and showed him a piece of money, the coin of the emperor, the head of the state, Jesus answered that we should give to Satan what belongs to Satan: "Give to Caesar what belongs to Caesar and to God what belongs to God" (Matt. 22:21).

TODAY THERE ARE two different ways that both are pledged to the fight against Mammon. One is the way of socialism and communism. The other way is the new way of communal work and fellowship in things spiritual and material.

This second way involves the voluntary, independent gathering together of people who are free of private property and capital. It is the way of the organic growth of the germ cell, the way of the seed that sprouts in a stony field: Here and there a little leaf tip shows through, and after a few days of sun and rain have passed, you can lie on the ground and see a great field of living shoots. Then a few weeks later, you will see a whole field of flourishing life, where even amid weeds and stones the young crop breaks through; what the

> Already now we can live in the power of this future, shaping our lives in the presence of the coming God, in accordance with the future kingdom. The kingdom of love, free of Mammon, is approaching this earth.

individual blade of wheat cannot achieve, the whole field can. Then harvest time is here: "Pray that laborers may be sent out into the harvest" (Matt. 9:37–38).

Here we see a great difference between the second way and the first, that of socialism and communism. Before the harvest, the wheat and the weeds are not to be separated, as Jesus warned in his well-known parable (Matt. 13:24–30). When a violent revolution seizes the servants of Mammon and hangs them from lamp-posts, aiming to leave alive only those who are communal-minded, it violates the spirit of Jesus. As he might have told the revolutionaries of his own day: *You should have waited until harvest time! You have torn out much wheat while still leaving weeds standing.*

In a violent revolution, Mammon simply passes from the hands of some to those of others. So when today we hear of fellow Christians being shot by the Bolshevik government for giving witness to the unity of humanity, we take our stand with these brothers and sisters. We have no part in armed revolution. Because it sheds blood, it is on the side of the Father of Lies (John 8:44). Our socialist brothers are deceiving themselves if they think they can overcome Mammon by arming themselves, that is, by relying on the same spirit of the abyss as Mammon itself. Poison cannot be cured with poison. Life can only be born of life, love of love, community of the will to community.

Our way to the goal of community is this second way. We walk the communal way of brotherliness and sisterliness, where small groups of people will meet, ready to be merged in the one goal, to belong to the one future.

Already now we can live in the power of this future, shaping our lives in the presence of the coming God, in accordance with the future kingdom. The victory of the Spirit manifests itself through the church community. The kingdom of love, free of Mammon, is approaching this earth. As the Gospel tells us: The kingdom of God has come very close. Change your thinking radically. Change radically so that you will be ready for the coming order of things.

> Come now, you rich people, weep and wail for the miseries that are coming to you. Your riches have rotted, and your clothes are moth-eaten. Your gold and silver have rusted, and their rust will be evidence against you, and it will eat your flesh like fire. You have laid up treasure during the last days. Listen! The wages of the laborers who mowed your fields, which you kept back by fraud, cry out, and the cries of the harvesters have reached the ears of the Lord of hosts. You have lived on the earth in luxury and in pleasure; you have nourished your hearts in a day of slaughter. You have condemned and murdered the righteous one, who does not resist you.
>
> Be patient, therefore, brothers and sisters, until the coming of the Lord. (James 5:1–7) ⇾

by Maria Weiss

Leper Colony Sketches

*A young woman finds pain and friendship
in an enforced community of outcasts.*

MARIA WEISS *with* MAUREEN BURN

MARIA WEISS WAS BORN IN BAVARIA *in 1900
and moved to South America as a child with her
family, growing up on farming properties between
Argentina and Paraguay. In 1928, she married
Adolfo, the son of neighboring immigrants, and
moved to his small farm in Argentina. They had
a son, Erwin. After five years they realized that
Maria was starting to develop symptoms of leprosy.*

*At the time, lepers were required to live in an
isolated colony, and the nearest one was across the
border in Sapucay, Paraguay. Adolfo had no choice
but to drive Maria there and leave her, returning
to their little son, knowing they might never see
one another again. Years later, Maria recounted
her experiences to a friend, Maureen Burn, who
recorded and translated them from the Spanish.*

A LONG TIME PASSED in which my only wish was to die and forget my misery. I had lost faith in everything. I believed neither in God nor the devil, and I never thought of the Bible anymore. I thought, what good had it been? It hadn't saved me from all this. I had quite forgotten how to smile and was more like a log than a living person.

Anastasia was very kind to me. She brought me my food and never pressed me to do any work in return for it. She said I could help her with the work if I wished, but I didn't wish to do anything. I just sat there pining for my husband and child. I must have continued like this for a couple of years.

Then one day when I was sitting out in the shade of a tree, a stranger came up to me and shook my hand and said, "How are you, Doña Maria?"

I wondered how he knew my name, so I looked at his face and recognized the keen young evangelist who had first told me about the Bible years before. His eyes were the same, though he was no longer so young.

I said, "I am very unhappy."

He said, "Seek for Jesus Christ," and he left me without another word.

I thought, "What a strange thing to say, and not a word of sympathy!" I went indoors and rooted out my Bible from the bottom of my trunk. I opened it and tried to read it but could not make head or tail of it. When Eugenio saw me with it, he said, "There is a group that reads the Bible every Sunday morning. They are Protestants of all kinds, and anyone can go and ask them to explain it."

So I went. The group met at the hut of a man called Apolinario. He welcomed me and told me I could come any time, and he gave me the present of a bombilla. He said I should learn to take maté with it. It was a good pastime, it was wholesome, and it would mix well with my thoughts about my husband and my son, and God.

[A bombilla is a metal straw with a built-in sieve. Yerba maté is a caffeinated drink brewed from dried leaves of a South American holly species.]

I found that to be true, and I began to go every Sunday to the gathering, and I began to understand bits of the Bible, the way Apolinario explained it. And then I began slowly to come alive again. I stopped sitting about, and I began to help Anastasia with her work.

I DID NOT LEARN all this at once, but bit by bit, as I began to forget my own sorrows and look around me. I went regularly to the gathering on Sunday morning, and I felt something strong and helpful in Apolinario. He was happy and had a trust in God, in spite of his very advanced state of the disease. This interested me so I asked him to tell me the story of his life.

Apolinario had been a soldier in the Chaco War (1932–1935). He was a devout Roman Catholic and practiced his religion conscientiously. He had seriously studied the Roman Catholic catechism, but he found something lacking. The thing he was looking for was a direct way to God without any priest or other man being necessary as a go-between. He was badly wounded and spent many months in hospital in Asunción. A Salvation Army woman used to come round the ward, visiting the patients and giving out Bibles to any who were interested. He took one and read it with

All illustrations by Maria Weiss. *Above*, Adolfo and Maria's wedding.

Summer 2023 51

deepening interest, for he thought it certainly spoke of a direct way to God, with Jesus the only mediator to show the way. He put a lot of questions to the woman, and she said they believed the way he did.

So Apolinario decided he wanted to put his life straight with God and with man. This caused him a bitter and painful struggle, which tore him for weeks, for he knew what the consequences would be if he confessed what he had been hiding. So he confessed that he had leprosy. He also felt he should marry his *compañera*, who was mother of his three children, even though he now had to leave and go to the newly opened leper colony at Sapucay.

EVER SINCE THEN, Apolinario had been trying to pass on to others what he had found. He held a little group of Protestants together and helped many to find a new strength and overcoming of their sorrow through faith. This often meant teaching people to read, so that they could read the Bible. But he would always tell them, "A man can only teach another a little bit about the Bible. The true teacher is the Spirit of God in the believer's heart. He will show you the meaning more and more, as you trust Him more and more in your life. Then you will find the Bible is an endless treasure house – you will always get something new out of it that you did not see before. It will become a lamp to your feet."

AFTER THE MEETING on Sunday morning at Apolinario's hut, we used to have some fine talks. Apolinario was especially glad to welcome unbelievers. They often said they found no attraction in religion, as religious folk were often so sour-faced. "Oh," said Apolinario, "that is unfortunately true, but such people are not yet free of the hold of the devil." Some people were surprised when they heard this, but Apolinario continued, "Very few people realize that it is the good folk who are the devil's working-ground. He is kept busy working on them. He does not need to bother about folk who just live for their lusts. He has them already in his kingdom, and he can leave them in peace, as they don't know he exists. But as soon as man begins to think, 'Perhaps there is a God,' then he begins to know there is a devil also. The man may think he is out of the devil's power, because he has stopped sinning, but as soon as he goes about in fear of the power of evil, he is still lassoed. Some good people are always on the lookout for evil and see evil possibilities in everything, so they frighten away the young with their sour looks. If only they knew how dangerous it is to think of the devil without each time thinking of God, to let your mind so dwell on evil that you forget that God is the stronger! The only way to cut free from the devil's lasso is to cut the bonds of fear, in faith in Christ's victory."

I HEARD OF A HOUSE that was cheap, as it was in such bad repair. I got a letter writer to write and ask my husband if he could help me buy it, which he did. The disadvantage of this house was that it was near the edge of the colony, so I found I was robbed of anything I left lying about outside. I lost my cooking pot, and I even lost my big feather eiderdown, which I had brought with me from home. I had hung it on my line to air in the sunshine.

But one good thing was that I was near a wood and could collect a nice big pile of firewood. I used

to take my axe and go out for the day or just for the morning. But one day I was so pleased with myself for chopping such a nice pile of wood that I forgot to bring my axe home with me. That was a big loss; I asked a man living nearby if he had seen it. He said, "What will you give me if I find it for you?"

Often you heard people say, "*Nadie hace ni un pelo sin dinero.*" (No one will do the least bit without pay.) This was said about the rich as well as about the poor. I was once collecting sow thistle outside the patio of a very fine house. The owner came out and said, "How much will you pay me for that?" But I went off and left her with her sow thistle weeds, which she could not use herself, as she had no pig.

ONE DAY IN THE MEAT QUEUE the folk were laughing about Don Federico's latest joke. Don Federico was very learned. He had lots of newspapers sent to him, because he wanted to know all that was happening in the world. For the past months his whole talk had been about the atom bomb, which he said was a terrible and crazy thing. He said that if an atom bomb were to fall on the colony, it would be a blessing – everyone would be cured in a flash!

Candido, a student, was standing next to me in the queue. He sometimes came to Apolinario's hut. I turned to him and said, "I am a *tonta* (stupid person). I can't figure out what an atom bomb is like." "You don't need to figure it out," he said. "It is just what happens when you have bigger and better wars. But the root of all wars is the same – greed and envy."

I thought about that. I didn't know anything about war, but I knew plenty about greed and envy, not only in rich people, but also in very poor people.

The man from whom I had bought my house had been a poor man and unable to do any repairs. I could understand that, but I could not understand why he had slashed and cut anything he could not uproot and take with him. He had even cut down two lovely creepers by the patio, because they would not transplant. They were lying on the ground withered. One was a beautiful mauve passionflower in bloom, and the other was *Sábado tarde* (Saturday afternoon), which has a beautiful scent and is used instead of perfume, though the flowers are greenish and not beautiful.

However, the creepers both began to grow again and made a nice bit of shade for my patio, and such a beautiful scent from the *Sábado tarde*! So I was very glad.

Another time I saw a man move to another house in the colony, and he went round squashing all his ripening pumpkins. I could not understand, so I asked him why he was wasting them like that.

"Oh," he said, "they won't ripen if I pick them and take them with me; they're too green yet."

"But why don't you leave them for the next man who will be living there?"

"I don't want another man to gain by my labors," he said. "I planted them. I looked after and watered them."

"Well," I said, "what about all the hungry pigs that wander around looking for something to eat? Couldn't you have left the pumpkins for them?"

"I don't want another man's pigs to fatten on my labor," he said. So we said no more about it.

That spirit is the root of war. It is very strong, but God is stronger.

[Some years later, Maria was recovering in the women's hospital wing after an illness.]

I HAD ASKED MY NEIGHBOR, Mauricio, what would be a fair price for my calf that day when I went to visit my animals. He said, "Seven hundred *guaranís*." Mauricio was the young man who could not be false or hypocritical, and I trusted him completely.

I told the women in the hospital that evening that I hoped to sell my calf for seven hundred *guaranís*. The news must have spread fast, for the very next morning Braulia came running to the hospital from her house at the far side of the colony. She came to ask if I would let her have the calf for one hundred *guaranís* down and the rest in slow stages later. I knew Braulia well, because I

had lived with her and her brother Julio and their mother Felipa when they were children and when I had no home of my own.

Now Braulia was married and very badly off. Her husband was a guitarist, and he found it hard to earn a living now that gramophones were taking the place of harps and guitars in the colony. I also had noticed that wives of musicians had all the heavy and rough outdoor work to do, for their husbands had to keep their hands soft and smooth. I felt sorry for Braulia and let her have the calf for one hundred *guaranís* down and the rest later.

The women in the hospital had been listening to our conversation, and when Braulia had gone, they came up to me and said, "You've made a bad bargain there" or "You'll never see the rest of the money" or "Don't you know that pair are a couple of thieves?" But they were wrong, for Braulia paid me the full sum in time.

These comments of the women in the hospital did not upset me in the least, but I had two visitors at the time: Catalina, who had come with some copies of *Arco Iris* for me, and Eminencia, who asked if she could live with me for a bit. Catalina said, "You'd better let me keep the hundred *guaranís* for you, or you will give them away," and Eminencia added, "Or you will lose them."

I was quite offended and said, "No, I can keep them safely myself." So they went, and I tied the money in the corner of a white head kerchief that I had. Then I went home to get a second bed put up for Eminencia. The next day was Sunday, and

Florenciana came to see if I was well enough to go to the meeting with her. She said, "Hurry, or we'll be late." It was a hot day, so I put on my kerchief to protect my head and neck. I walked so fast that I got too hot and pushed the kerchief back off my head and forgot about it. After the meeting, when it was time to go back to the hospital, I noticed it was missing, with the money still tied in one corner! I looked everywhere in and around my hut and asked at all the houses on the way back to the hospital if anyone had seen it, and they all said no.

When I got back, already a few people were waiting for me. News had got around that I had some money, and one after another, people came to borrow some.

I told them I had none. "But you got a hundred *guaranís* yesterday," they said. "Yes," I said, "but I've spent it." Then I realized I had lied. It had all happened so quickly, and I had not meant to lie. And I thought how cunning the devil was to make me do it, when I wanted to live telling the truth.

Then I saw in a flash how he had managed it. He made me proud. I did not want the women to laugh at me and say, "There now, we told you so!" So I lied. And I remembered that the devil himself had fallen by pride, so he knows very well how to use pride to make others stumble and fall. I felt cast down about myself, but I knew I could forget myself and my failings by getting a fresh look at our Lord. This I found to be true, and I was also set free from my self-despondency, so as to think of others who might need a helping hand.

anymore but trusted them to his hands, for I knew he could care for them better than I could.

And I began to realize how many things I would not have known if I had stayed happily at home, with husband, son, house, and farm, and kith and kin nearby. For at the colony I was forced to find strength and comfort in the Bible and the hymnal.

I had also learned that God can come and give a joy such as I had never heard of when I had all the things around me that folk prize most in life – husband, child, and home.

WHEN I CAME BACK to my hut, I made myself a maté and sat in the shade of the creeper by my door and sucked the bombilla Apolinario had given me so many years ago, when I first went to his gatherings. He had told me the bombilla would be a good pastime and would mix well with my thoughts.

In my more active days I did not linger for hours with my maté bombilla, but I always liked maté. I found it warmed you when you were cold and cooled you when you were hot, and it gave you fresh energy when you were tired.

And I found now that it was truer than ever that the bombilla mixed well with my thoughts. But I found my thoughts had completely changed since those early days in the colony. Then my thoughts were entirely about me or about mine. I was sorry for myself, and it was always a case of "poor me," and I worried endlessly about my husband and my son.

Now I hardly ever thought about myself. I often used to think I had little more education than one of my hens, but I knew that just as God had cared for me all these years, so he could care for my husband and child also. So I did not worry

AFTER EIGHTEEN YEARS, Maria was reunited with her husband and son, who had meanwhile joined the Bruderhof's Primavera community about one hundred miles north of Sapucay.

Immigrants who were expelled from Germany in the early years of Hitler's regime, Bruderhof members had built up three communities in eastern Paraguay, which were in existence from 1941 to 1961. They also ran a hospital for the surrounding area; it was here that Maria was flown in a small plane in 1954, for an operation. She was welcomed to stay, living in semi-isolation by the hospital until it was clear that her leprosy was in abeyance, and then joining the life and daily activities of the community together with her husband and son, to their great joy. Maria died in a Bruderhof community in Connecticut in 1988. ➤

Maria Weiss's story is told in her book, Outcast But Not Forsaken: True Stories from a Paraguayan Leper Colony *(Plough), a journal narrative based on conversations with Maureen Burn.*

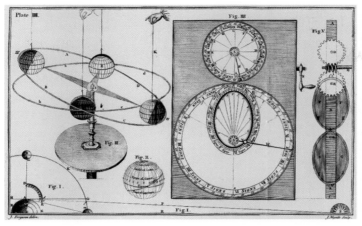

James Ferguson, *Distance Of Sun, Moon, & Planets*, 1756

Argument of Periapsis

The angle between the ascending node of an orbiting body and its periapsis,
the point at which it is closest to the gravitational center of another body,
measured in the direction of orbital motion.   —Dr. Alice Gorman

We argued again today. This time? It might
have been a pot unwashed, or trash day missed—
I can't remember—a stupid, pointless fight
as if controlled by some ventriloquist.

Slam door, start car, and leave, radio blaring.
On the highway, I head north, nowhere to go
but through the night sky, muttering and swearing.
I drive too fast to the next exit, then slow

and circle back.
                Just barely healed, we're shy,
quiet and tentative, making our way
together. Is there sound in space? We try
saying what we really mean to say.

I cannot travel very far from you—
yours is the body I am closest to.

MIDGE GOLDBERG

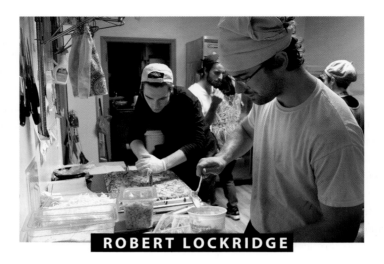

ROBERT LOCKRIDGE

Pay As You Can

*At a café where we grow the food and don't name a price,
we're still learning new mindsets.*

SO, FRIENDS, every day do something
that won't compute. Love the Lord.
Love the world. Work for nothing.
Take all that you have and be poor.
—*Wendell Berry, "Manifesto:
The Mad Farmer Liberation Front"*

CRACKING THREE EGGS over the griddle and tossing their shells in the compost, I glimpse Kevin and his friend as they step past folks in line, slide up beside the pay-as-you-can sign, and launch directly into placing their order.

"They have the best coffee," Kevin tells his friend, then turns to me. "I tell everyone you guys have the best coffee in town. I need a cup of that good, fresh coffee, and a waffle with whipped cream and fruit, and eggs with cheese, and one of those buns, and . . . "

Pirouetting around the galley kitchen, I interrupt: "Good morning, Kevin. I'll be with you in just a minute."

I pivot back to my tasks: plate a breakfast stir-fry, flip the eggs, grind the direct-trade coffee, prime the waffle maker, spread cream cheese and Sungold-tomato jelly over a homemade garlic rosemary bagel for Emily, a regular sitting at the bar, and then ask Meredith to dress a few more cinnamon buns and crabapple scones. Despite my efforts to keep my emotions in check, my heart has galloped up under my collar and refuses to settle back into my chest.

Kevin, who frequents the café most days we're open, always greets me with an easy grin and cheerful conversation as he ambles through the entrance after tying his dog, Molly, outside, where she waits patiently for him. I enjoy seeing him and can usually bottle the frustration that bubbles up when his food orders snowball into long lists that include a waffle and eggs for Molly, several

---

Robert Lockridge lives in Norwood, Ohio, with his wife, Erin, and their two children. With Matt Latchaw and Lyric Morris-Latchaw they have coauthored The Moriah Pie Cookbook: Stories and Recipes from a Life of Parish Farming *(Wipf and Stock, 2022).*

to-go containers, and phrases like "and throw in a couple of those."

Most of the time, I am mysteriously enlivened by all of the "foolish" work behind this pay-as-you-can, neighborhood-grown breakfast café – by doing something that, in Wendell Berry's words, "won't compute" with the economics of the world. And even for the less inspiring parts – like when the baking regimen that begins at 3:30 a.m. compounds the sleep deprivation that comes with having young children – the work still makes a deep-down, bedrock sort of sense to me. But this morning, I feel vulnerable. The café has been slow lately, we have been losing money, and I am exhausted. I remind myself that I signed up for this arrangement, but with my heart thundering in my ears, I fear that Kevin and his friend's "usual" is going to be more than I know how to offer.

Turning back to them, pen and paper in hand, I offer a half-hearted "good morning" and begin taking their orders. Along with many paying patrons, there are a handful of regulars who pay little or nothing for their breakfasts, which are usually reasonable, single-entree orders with a cup of coffee. This is exactly what my wife, Erin, and I had in mind when we first opened Moriah Pie, the pay-as-you-can pizza restaurant we ran for eight years before switching the format to this breakfast café. We wanted to share the food that we grew here in our urban neighborhood with the people who live here, whether or not they could afford it. We wanted to trust in God's provision, opening the table to anyone who wanted a seat. But as Kevin and his friend order enough food to feed six people, a dam breaks within me. Putting down my pen on the counter, I can't help but say something.

"Hey guys, I'm going to remind you again how this works."

Kevin interrupts, "I gotcha, I gotcha, you know I always take care of you."

I try to remain blind to what people pay, but having previously encouraged him to pay *something*, he has on occasion handed me an envelope of pennies, the change he no longer wants to carry in his pocket. I do not feel "taken care of" by Kevin.

Holding up an egg, my hand shaking, I say, "Kevin, this egg here costs me $0.38. That coffee that you love costs me $11 a pound. Your friend Jared here will be washing dishes in a few minutes and I pay him $11 an hour. That money has to come from somewhere. I rely on you and all the people here to pay him, to pay the rent, to buy the groceries, and to take care of my family. If you guys have money for weed or beer, you need to have some for us too. I am busting my butt and I don't feel like you are honoring me or my family."

My whole body is lurching with the release of adrenaline. Having been as real as I know how to be, I turn back to the griddle. Later, calmer now, I walk over to Kevin's table with to-go containers and reiterate that I value his presence at the café. He tells me that he will be picking up some hours at a temp job that afternoon and will pay me some real money next week. There is an honesty between us that I haven't felt in a long time.

Three weeks have passed, and I haven't seen Kevin again. I'm sure I could have spoken with more eloquence or compassion. Had I simply named a price, the whole situation could have been avoided. Had I remained bottled up, Kevin would have gone on with his day. But I would have grown hard of heart and he would have continued to take this "free" meal for granted. We would have reduced each other to commodities – something flat, rather than people who reflect the face of God.

So as messy as it felt, I'm glad I lost my cool. At every turn, often without our awareness, we are conditioned to receive the world around us as commodity. As a result, our senses are dulled to the gifts of creation, one another, and God's dynamic provision. If we are to re-apprehend the world as gift, we must wrestle through this temptation, by engaging in real and often messy relationships. Ten years into this work, I am still learning how to do it well. ⌁

Julia Stankova, *The Anointing of Christ*, painting on canvas, 2009

In Praise of
Costly Magnificence

Mary of Bethany shows the beauty of extravagance.

ALASTAIR ROBERTS

THE STORY IS WELL KNOWN, though not as well as, according to Jesus, it should be. It's around the time of what would later be called Holy Week. Jesus is in Bethany, a town two miles or so from Jerusalem, where he has friends. One of them, a man called Simon the Leper, hosts a dinner for him and his disciples. Others are invited as well: notably, Lazarus, who not very long before this had been dead, whom Jesus had raised from his tomb, and Martha and Mary, Lazarus' sisters. Lazarus is reclining at the table. Martha, as is typical with her, is serving; Mary, as is typical with her, is doing something else.

She comes into the dining room, carrying something. She opens it: it's a jar, filled with "about a pound of expensive ointment made from pure nard." She pours it on Jesus' head, and on his feet to anoint them, wiping his feet with her hair. Judas, among others, rebukes her for this extravagance, and Jesus rebukes him for his rebuke: "Leave her alone. Why do you trouble her? She has done a beautiful thing to me. For you always have the poor with you, and whenever you want, you can do good for them. But you will not always have me. She has done what she could; she has anointed my body beforehand for burial. And truly, I say to you, wherever the gospel is proclaimed in the whole world, what she has done will be told in memory of her."

It's a brief, strange, powerful story that points to a reality at the center of the world, as it is transformed and set right again by Christ: the importance and inner meaning of the virtue of magnificence, and the relationship between money and love.

The accounts of the anointing of Jesus at the meal in Bethany (Matt. 26:6–13; Mark 14:3–9; John 12:1–8) are pivotal to the drama and laden with the thematic import of their respective gospels. My paraphrase above is a sort of harmonization,

Alastair Roberts received his PhD from Durham University and teaches for both the Theopolis Institute and the Davenant Institute. He participates in the Mere Fidelity *and* Theopolis *podcasts. He and his wife,* Plough *editor Susannah Black Roberts, split their time between New York City and the United Kingdom.*

but there are differences between the accounts. Indeed, reading commentaries on the Gospel accounts of the anointing, one typically finds extensive discussion of their similarities, contrasts, and relationship, as well as consideration of whether Luke's account of the sinful woman (Luke 7:36–50) is a contrasting record of the same historical occurrence. Illuminating and useful though such discussions can be, preoccupation with questions of harmonization and historicity can dull hearers' attention to ways the Gospel writers have crafted their accounts to foreground distinctive themes and connections. Alertness to these themes and connections can relieve some of the perceived inconsistencies and tensions between them.

The Olivet Discourse directly precedes both Matthew's and Mark's accounts of the anointing at Bethany, while the accounts of Judas' betrayal of Jesus to the chief priests and the Last Supper immediately follow. At first glance, their temporal setting of the event differs from that of John – his takes place six days before the Passover, rather than two (John 12:1; Matt. 26:2; Mark 14:1). By virtue of its narrative setting, however, Mary's anointing Jesus plays a pivotal role in Matthew and Mark, seemingly provoking Judas to his betrayal. If one takes Matthew and John together, Judas is reacting specifically to Jesus' praise of Mary and the rebuke of his own suggestion that the nard might be more sensibly and usefully disposed of – "Why was this ointment not sold for three hundred denarii and given to the poor?" – when he goes to the chief priests and asks them to make him an offer: "What will you give me if I deliver him over to you?" Indeed, we might speculate that Matthew and Mark, in speaking of "when Jesus was at Bethany" (Matt. 26:6; Mark 14:3) were referring to an earlier event, a flashback in the narrative that provides critical background for Judas' betrayal two days before the Passover.

The actions of the woman with the nard, unnamed in Matthew's and Mark's accounts, are treated as prophetic or anticipatory of Jesus' burial. He lauds her in the highest possible terms: "Truly, I say to you, wherever this gospel is proclaimed in the whole world, what she has done will also be told in memory of her" (Matt. 26:13). Her astonishing action, so scandalous to Judas, both provokes his betrayal and is contrasted with it. The perfume was incredibly costly, three hundred denarii by Mark's and John's accounts (Mark 14:5; John 12:5) – nearly a year's wages for a typical laborer.

Mary's extravagant action (matched in the immense and costly quantity of burial spices used by Joseph of Arimathea and Nicodemus in John 19:39), condemned as a waste of money by Judas and others of the disciples, is praised as a "beautiful thing" by Jesus. The Gospel writers further accent the righteous character of her actions by contrasting them with the character and actions of Judas. John records the protest as coming from the mouth of Judas, while revealing that Judas was a thief, who did not truly regard the poor as he feigned. Matthew and Mark, by connecting and juxtaposing the two events, invite their hearers to consider the jarring contrast between the costly and loving anointing of Jesus and Judas' callous and mercenary sale of him: Thirty pieces of silver is the cost of a slave. (cf. Exod. 21:32; Zech. 11:12–13).

John's account of the anointing is situated before Jesus' triumphal entry into Jerusalem and is associated with events different from those in Matthew and Mark. John's is the one that names her: neither Mary nor Martha is named more generally in Matthew or Mark. John's account of the anointing immediately follows his account of the raising of Lazarus; he seems concerned that we connect them. Within his account of the raising of Lazarus in chapter 11, John disrupts the narrative, introducing Mary by referring to her later actions in chapter 12 ("It was Mary who anointed the Lord with ointment and wiped his feet with her hair, whose brother Lazarus was ill" – John 11:2). And chapter 12 recalls the events of the preceding chapter: "Six days before the Passover, Jesus therefore came to Bethany, where Lazarus was, whom Jesus had raised from the dead."

The death of Lazarus and his raising are presented in the Gospel with tenderness and pain: "Jesus loved Martha and her sister and Lazarus," John tells us directly; to his disciples, Jesus refers to Lazarus as "our friend." Mary weeps before leading him to the site of her brother's burial; Jesus himself weeps at the violation, this horror of death; he is, we are told twice, "greatly moved." But details emerge as we read the whole story: Mary had wept *at Jesus' feet*; Martha had been worried that, in opening Lazarus's tomb, they would encounter *the odor of death*. And

Julia Stankova, *The Raising of Lazarus*, painting on wood, 2022

then there was the raising, this superabundant act, which brings into the present the promise of the future resurrection: Jesus loves this family, and he will not allow death the victory here. Not this time, not to these loved ones. In placing the raising of Lazarus and Mary's anointing of Jesus alongside each other, narrating each with an explicit reference to the other, and accentuating both common and contrasting details in his accounts, John encourages his hearers to attend both to the ways that Mary's anointing of Jesus follows from the raising of Lazarus and the ways it is illuminated by it.

In John's account the motives for the anointing are clearly implied: the immense love and gratitude of a woman whose brother Jesus had raised from death (perhaps the identification of Mary in 11:2 suggests that, although her anointing of Jesus was well known, some of John's hearers may not have known what occasioned it). The love that motivated Mary's action is perhaps further heightened by John's evocation of Song of Songs 1:12 – "While the king was on his couch, my nard gave forth its fragrance."

Read against the backdrop of the story of the raising of Lazarus, other facets of the anointing come to the fore. The nard-scented air that fills the house contrasts with the stench of the tomb. But we might also see Jesus' statements concerning his coming burial in a new light. Jesus' claim that Mary is preparing his body for burial is jarring when we consider that her action is one of overwhelming gratitude to Jesus for raising her brother from death. Why refer to the grave just where we might have thought we were celebrating its defeat? Perhaps because the deliverance of Lazarus from his tomb is integrally related to Jesus' descent into his.

Our sense that John wants us to meditate upon such questions should be heightened by the events of the following chapter, which recall the anointing at Bethany:

> Now before the Feast of the Passover, when Jesus knew that his hour had come to depart out of this world to the Father, having loved his own who were in the world, he loved them to the end. During supper, when the devil had already put it into the heart of Judas Iscariot, Simon's son, to betray him, Jesus, knowing that the Father had given all things into his hands, and that he had come from God and was going back to God, rose from supper. He laid aside his outer garments, and taking a towel, tied it around his waist. Then he poured water into a basin and began to wash the disciples' feet and to wipe them with the towel that was wrapped around him. (John 13:1–5)

Whereas the synoptic Gospels present the institution of the Eucharist as the symbolic act related to Jesus' coming death in the context of the Last Supper, John does not record it. Uniquely among the Gospels, John tells of Jesus washing his disciples' feet, which fulfills some measure of the same purpose; it is, as you might say, the same "beat" in the story. By focusing his account on Mary's anointing the feet of Jesus, in contrast to Matthew and Mark, which focus upon his head, John's narrative accents similarities between Mary's anointing of Jesus' feet and Jesus' washing of his disciples' feet.

Jesus' washing of his disciples' feet is presented as an act of loving service, a remarkable action which the disciples will not truly understand until a later time (John 13:1, 7). The anointing at Bethany anticipated his burial, but his washing

Julia Stankova, *Christ Washes his Disciples' Feet*, painting on wood, 2022

of the disciples' feet seems to be a symbol of his loving service in laying down his life for them. If Mary scandalized the disciples with her extravagance, Jesus scandalized them by humbling himself on account of his love for them. In both cases, the disciples reveal their inability to perceive the lavish love at the heart of the gospel: the love of Christ for them and the answering love of those who have experienced the wonder of that love.

The prodigality of Mary of Bethany's loving act is memorialized as an integral element of the narrative of the gospel itself and by Jesus' own declared desire (Matt. 26:13). While we might perhaps consider her act excessive, Jesus praises it as profoundly fitting, even paradigmatic. Indeed, juxtaposed as sharply as it is with Judas' mercenary betrayal of his Lord, perhaps Mary's anointing is singled out for an immortality that is the inverse of his infamy.

Attitudes to money lie near the heart of the contrast between Mary and Judas' actions. What do we believe about money? Reading other parts of the New Testament, it might be easy to assume that money is chiefly to be considered as a dangerous power from whose idolatrous control we need to free our imaginations and desires. Jesus speaks of "unrighteous mammon" (Luke 16:11) and instructs the rich young ruler to sell all he has and distribute to the poor (Luke 18:22). The New Testament frequently warns us against the love of money, "a root of all kinds of evils" (1 Tim. 6:10; cf. Heb. 13:5). Money, it might seem, is a crushing weight upon our souls, from which we need to release ourselves.

The poor are singled out as the primary recipients of God's grace in the New Testament (e.g. Luke 6:20; 7:22), while the rich are typically characterized by spiritual blindness and insensibility (Luke 12:16–21; 16:13–14, 19–31) and are the recipients of woes. "But woe to you who are rich, for you have received your consolation. Woe to you who are full now, for you shall be hungry.

Woe to you who laugh now, for you shall mourn and weep." (Luke 6:24–25). "It is easier for a camel to go through the eye of a needle than for a rich person to enter the kingdom of God" (Matt. 19:24). "Has not God chosen those who are poor in the world to be rich in faith and heirs of the kingdom, which he has promised to those who love him?" (James 2:5).

The accumulation of great wealth is commonly associated with oppression of the poor. James describes the rich as the oppressors of the church (James 2:6–7) and of their workers, who will be avenged by the Lord (5:1–5). In his judgment upon the temple, Jesus foregrounds the figure of a poor widow, who gives all the money she has to the temple funds (Luke 21:1–4), immediately after he has condemned the wealthy scribes for devouring widows' houses (Luke 20:46–47). When the rich tax collector Zacchaeus repents, the first thing he does is to give half of his goods to the poor and restore fourfold to any he had defrauded. Indeed, Jesus charges his disciples to sell their possessions and give to the poor (Luke 12:33).

Against all this background, Jesus' celebration of Mary's act might puzzle us. Putting to one side his motives as a thief, surely Judas' protest was justified: Mary's anointing of Jesus with the costly perfume was a wasteful act, imprudent, extravagant, even luxurious. The money should have been given to the poor instead. This, however, is to miss the animating heart of Jesus' teaching, which was never *chiefly* the negative character of wealth, the injustice of economic inequality, our need to divest ourselves of our wealth, and to redistribute to the poor. Such beliefs can all too easily be driven by a spirit of envy and ressentiment, no less under the thrall of money and its kingdom of values. Judas had never escaped this, as his judgment of Mary's action reveals.

What Mary sees, that Judas and the disciples miss, is that our attitude to money must be guided by – simply *is* shaped by, if we are perceiving the world aright – love's recognition of the all-surpassing worth of the kingdom of God, and the One in whom it is present in person. The danger of money lies in the ways love of it can seduce our hearts from the One who exceeds all else in value. Recognizing this, much of the New Testament teaching concerning money should fall into place. Jesus' charge to the rich young ruler and to his disciples to sell and give to the poor was in order that they might have treasure in heaven and freely follow him, with hearts loosed into joyful generosity by the sense of abundance that they have found in him. Jesus speaks of something similar in a pair of parables in Matthew 13:44–46:

> The kingdom of heaven is like treasure hidden in a field, which a man found and covered up. Then in his joy he goes and sells all that he has and buys that field.
>
> Again, the kingdom of heaven is like a merchant in search of fine pearls, who, on finding one pearl of great value, went and sold all that he had and bought it.

The apostle Paul speaks of this same surpassing value in Philippians 3:8:

> Indeed, I count everything as loss because of the surpassing worth of knowing Christ Jesus my Lord. For his sake I have suffered the loss of all things and count them as rubbish, in order that I may gain Christ.

Mary's act illuminates the radical transvaluation brought about by the love of Christ – the all-surpassing love that we have tasted and the answering love that rises in our hearts through his Spirit. And here we might begin to understand something of the significance of John's analogy between Mary's loving anointing of Jesus' feet and his washing of his disciples' feet. Jesus' washing of his disciples' feet manifests the reality of his coming death, his "taking the form of a servant" and humbling himself to the point of death on the cross (Phil. 2:5–8). This was an act of surpassing love: "For you know the grace of our Lord Jesus Christ, that though he was rich, yet for your sake he became poor, so that you by his poverty might become rich" (2 Cor. 8:9). What Paul says specifically in Philippians is that Jesus "emptied himself." He poured himself out with a lavish hand, in taking his servant's form and in dying. And by the love that alone can begin to fathom this marvelous self-gift, we will want to respond in kind.

The self-gift of our Lord is eternally memorialized, but the gift of Mary is remembered too. Unlike the man who would sell him for thirty pieces of silver, Mary recognized Jesus' incomparable value and acted accordingly. In the magnificent extravagance of her act, not motivated by the desire for praise – indeed, in the face of censure – Mary fittingly expresses this truth that the eyes of Christian love alone can see.

It is, in the most precise sense, a magnificent gesture. While the Aristotelian virtue of magnificence was largely restricted to the rich and powerful in the ancient world, Mary's act illustrates its place at the heart of Christian practice. Because we are children of a King, we can act like it, with a kind of prodigal generosity. We don't need to spend all our lives scrimping. We have enough; we have, in fact, everything. Mary exemplifies the joyful liberality of love's answer to unfathomable grace, a magnificence that is conformed to the immeasurable self-gift to which it responds.

For too many of us, money remains the ultimate measure of value, never having been eclipsed by Christ and his kingdom. The Victorian writer John Ruskin sought to expose some of the deep errors that arise when we treat money as the measure of all things. The only true value, Ruskin insisted, is life. Where riches are accumulated in the service of oppression, destruction, greed, and vice such "wealth" is utterly contrary to the "weal." In a powerful passage, Ruskin compares this to the flowing of water:

Wealth, therefore, is "the possession of the valuable by the valiant." . . . The two elements, the value of the thing, and the valour of its possessor, must be estimated together. Whence it appears that many of the persons commonly considered wealthy, are in reality no more wealthy than the locks of their own strong boxes are, they being inherently and eternally incapable of wealth; and operating . . . either as pools of dead water, and eddies in a stream . . . or else, as dams in a river, of which the ultimate service depends not on the dam, but the miller; or else, as mere accidental stays and impediments, acting not as wealth, but (for we ought to have a correspondent term) as "illth," causing various devastation and trouble around them in all directions; or lastly, act not at all, but are merely animated conditions of delay (no use being possible of anything they have until they are dead).

In the Gospel of John, similar motifs of flowing arise at several points. In John 4, in talking with the Samaritan woman at the well, Jesus offers living water that will become in its recipient "a spring of water welling up to eternal life" (verse 14). In chapter 7, in speaking of the Spirit that would be given at Pentecost, Jesus declares "out of his heart will flow rivers of living water" (verse 38). In recording the events of the crucifixion, John draws our attention to the fact that water mixed with blood flowed from Jesus' pierced side (19:34–35). Jesus' self-gift, his pouring out of his life for mankind, compared to water, makes its recipients into springs of living water themselves.

In answer to his disciples' rebuke of Mary, Jesus declares: "The poor you always have with you, but you do not always have me" (John 12:8). After the Ascension, it would no longer be possible to perform such a magnificent act as Mary performed upon Jesus' physical body. Yet Jesus still has a body on earth, toward which we can still express our love, which calls out for our magnificence. In Matthew 25, the chapter before

the anointing at Bethany is recorded, Jesus speaks of how loving deeds done towards "one of the least of these my brothers" are done to him (verses 31–46).

The pouring forth of life – true life – from Jesus produces a new economy, of which the magnificence of loving self-gifts such as Mary's is characteristic; her anointing of Jesus at Bethany is described in a way that evokes both the memory and anticipation of God's own gift of his Spirit. Elsewhere, when we read of something filling a house, it is almost invariably God's own presence

What Mary sees, that Judas and the disciples miss, is that our attitude to money must be guided by love's recognition of the all-surpassing worth of the kingdom of God, and the One in whom it is present in person.

by his Spirit (Exod. 40:34–35; 1 Kings 8:10–11; 2 Chron. 5:13–14; 7:2; Isa. 6:4; Ezek. 10:3–4; Acts 2:2). As the scent of her nard fills the house at Bethany, the Spirit of love is mysteriously manifest.

The one gift of the Spirit at Pentecost, poured out by the ascended Christ in loving magnificence, produces an "economy" of life in his body, as by many gifts of that one Spirit its members liberally minister the life that they have received to others. Paradoxically, this life is received in the act of giving. Like living water, it does not stand still or stagnate or get dammed up, but exuberantly flows from each to his neighbor, in countless tributaries of loving self-gift, from its source in the inexhaustible spring of Calvary. ⬎

The Last of the
Revolutionaries

What's left of the Cuban Revolution
seventy years after it began?

Photographs and Interviews by Harvey Maltese

ON JULY 26, 1953, Fidel Castro's rebel forces attacked the Moncada Barracks in Santiago de Cuba – the first shots fired in what became the Cuban Revolution. With each passing year the guerrillas who fought alongside Castro and Che Guevara are fewer. Many who survive continue to support the cause of the revolution unconditionally. Their children and grandchildren, especially those born during the economic crisis Cuba has faced since the collapse of the Soviet Union, see things differently. Those who haven't already left the island increasingly express frustration as the economic situation worsens and hope for a brighter future grows dim. Who are the revolutionaries now? I traveled to Cuba to ask both the old and young generations what they see as the revolution's legacy.　　　　　　　　 —*Harvey Maltese (pen name)*

Opposite, Isael, born in 1940 in the Sierra Maestra, joined the revolutionary forces at age sixteen and served for three years in Fidel Castro's bodyguard: "My life is all about being a revolutionary, and it will stay that way until I die." *Above,* Mailon, age twenty-four, Havana: "I am a revolutionary for my country, but a different kind from what the government promotes. To be a revolutionary is to defend what is yours in your country, but not because someone tells you to or forces you to do so."

Victor *(Alamar, Havana)*: I was fourteen years old when the revolution was declared. Growing up, I felt the Batista dictatorship in my own flesh – I saw the misery it caused. My dad was a union organizer in the sugar factory. He went to jail several times. We were poor. But after the revolution my father could own the house we lived in. I could get a scholarship, study in Havana.

I was always a revolutionary – back then most young people were. But today a lot of young people are influenced by the internet, where 90 percent of what you'll see is biased against countries like Cuba. It's a tough time. But although it's not easy, I'm happy being a revolutionary. It still lights up my soul.

Reinier *(Victor's son)*: Young people can see the world is changing. I agree that the revolution was great in the beginning, I think it turned into something different. I don't want to fight anybody and I don't want to ever carry weapons. Being a true revolutionary, for me, is to do things better, whatever you're doing. That's my revolution.

Fabian *(Centro Habana)*: I am twenty-six years old. I never went to university, I never had a proper job, I struggled to express myself verbally, and that's why I started painting. To try and tell my truth. To share my dream with people.

It's hard to dream in Cuba. Many people feel trapped. I don't think about the future much – it's about surviving each day at a time. If you look at the streets, things aren't going well. And even though revolution is supposed to be about change, about things getting better, we're still stuck in the past. Maybe because we weren't here before, the young need to make our own changes, our own revolution. But the older generations don't listen to the young.

I try to keep evolving, to learn as much as I can. And to treat other people well. That's my way of being a revolutionary – it's

Maria *(Santiago de la Vega, Havana)*: I saw the revolution begin when I was about twenty years old. It was late in 1956 when I saw a boat landing at the Playa Las Coloradas. An officer in Batista's army was there too. He told me, "Wait here, there are some rebels arriving." It was Fidel. I hid some of the rebel fighters in my home. Later, I left my home and went to the Sierra Maestra mountains where they were based. I gathered information about the movements of Batista's army.

What made me take the side of the revolution was the crisis ordinary Cubans were going through. We were hungry, our needs were neglected, and we felt abandoned by the government. I knew if Cuba didn't change my son would never go to school, never be properly fed, nothing. I became a revolutionary in those days. I am ninety now. I will stay a

Susel *(Maria's granddaughter)*: I am twenty-one years old. My grand-mother is a courageous person. Sometimes I think about all the hard times my father had to endure because of my grandmother's choices, and my feelings are more complicated. But most of the time I take strength from her courage. That's how the revolution was made, I think – through actions like those that my grandmother took back then.

There's a crisis for ordinary people today – different from the one my grandmother lived through, but still a crisis – and I'm trying to make a positive change in response, like she did. My boyfriend and I run a community project in the town where we live. We're starting a farm and building a space on it where artists and musicians can work. Whether it's painters, singers, or just people in the neighborhood, everyone is welcome.

Misael *(Granma Province)*: I was twenty when I joined the revolution. At the time, I worked with donkeys transporting merchandise. I was living here when Che Guevara came to the Sierra Maestra. I asked a rebel I knew to introduce me. That's how I became second-in-command of supplying Che's battalion. Che used to talk a lot with me about politics, which back then I didn't know anything about. I wanted to join the revolution because of the brutality of Batista's army. They killed my sister-in-law, and they tried to kill me, many times.

Later I went to Havana and Fidel made me a first lieutenant in his new army. But I didn't like the army. I told Che I was going back to the mountains to work with my donkeys again. He told me I was crazy. I went back anyway.

I am about to turn ninety-six. I still don't like politics. But being a revolutionary is still everything to me.

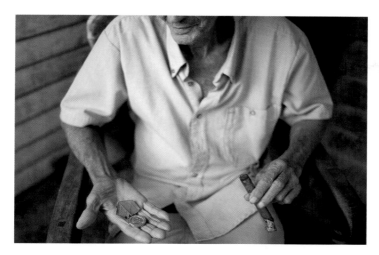

Raul *(Granma Province)*: I joined the revolution when I was fourteen years old. My family had a small farm, so we weren't the poorest of the poor, but I still had to work as a child – chopping sugar cane, selling charcoal. There was misery everywhere in Cuba – only those who lived through it can truly know. In my eyes, the revolution was truly great, because it swept all that away.

When a rebellion began in the Escambray Mountains against Fidel's new government, they called for volunteers to defend the revolution. I went into the mountains in 1961, as a scout, and stayed there for one and a half years. The mountains were filled with enemy fighters. There were many deaths.

I'm seventy-nine now, and I'm still a fighter, a *combatiente*. Even though I'm an old man now, I haven't changed. If it was necessary, I would go back and fight.

Luis *(Alamar, Havana)*: I am twenty-four and work as a pizza chef. My grandfather fought in the revolution when he was only seventeen years old. He followed his brother into the revolution, and he lost him in the war. Revolutions are about change, making a better world. And that was the dream that my grandfather and his brother fought for. But between then and now that dream got diverted, things went onto a different path, and in Cuba today I don't think you can see it any more. Nowadays the revolution is just some people hanging on to power.

And the people who fought for the dream are forgotten – people who fought in the Sierra Maestra, in the Escambray. They've been forgotten by the veterans' associations and by the government. If my grandfather didn't have my grandmother and his children, he'd be alone. If that's what happened to our elders who made the revolution, what will happen to us? *(Continued on the next page.)*

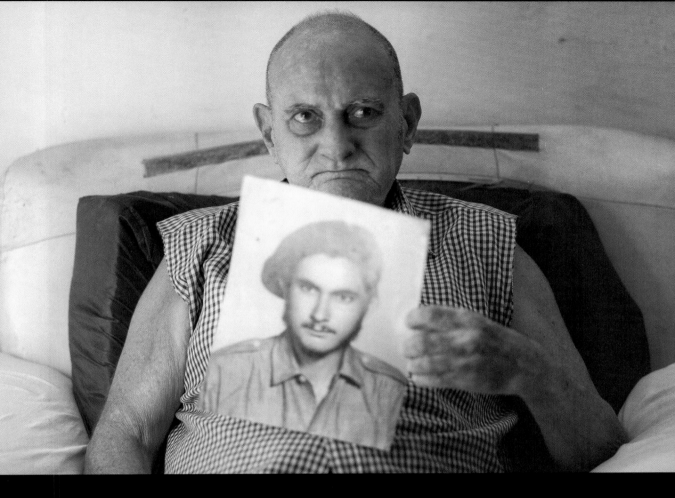

My grandfather helped make a big change in his time, a complete change. Everyone could learn to read and write, see a doctor, get an education. The revolution gave houses to many families that lived in terrible conditions under the dictatorship. And during the 1980s, thanks to the USSR, there was food, economic stability, jobs. But I was born in 1998, and I have only ever known black-outs, unemployment, bad transportation. Only problems, and the problems never get solved.

So many people are homeless – it feels like we're back to the days before the revolution. Maybe things are repeating themselves. We need a new perspective. The dream of the revolution was the dream of change, of going in a new direction. I think we have to do that again, take another turn, go onto another road. A road that will take us somewhere where no one is forgotten.

Ownership & Communion

*A sixteenth-century Anabaptist spells out
the economics of the Apostles' Creed.*

PETER RIEDEMANN

In 1542, Peter Riedemann, a Silesian shoemaker imprisoned by Prince Philip of Hesse as a leader of the communal Anabaptists, wrote to his captor arguing that scripture and the ecumenical creeds require common ownership. From Peter Riedemann's Confession of Faith:

ALL BELIEVERS HAVE FELLOWSHIP IN holy things, that is, in God.[1] He has given them all things in his Son, Christ Jesus.[2] Just as Christ has nothing for himself, since all he has is for us, so too, no members of Christ's body should possess any gift for themselves or for their own sake. Instead, all should be consecrated for the whole body, for all the members.[3] This is so because Christ also did not bring his gifts for one individual or the other, but for everyone, for the whole body.

Community of goods applies to both spiritual and material gifts. All of God's gifts, not only the spiritual but also the temporal, have been given so that they not be kept but be shared with each other. Therefore, the fellowship of believers should be visible not only in spiritual but also in temporal things.[4] Paul says one person should not have an abundance while another suffers want; instead, there should be equality.[5] This he shows by pointing to the law about manna. According to that rule, the one who gathered much had nothing extra, and the one who gathered little had no lack, since each was given the amount needed.[6]

Furthermore, the Creation still testifies today that at the beginning God ordained that people should own nothing individually but should have all things in common with each other.[7] However, by taking what they should have left, and by leaving what they should have taken,[8] people have gained possession of things and have become more accustomed to accumulating things and hardened in doing so. Through such appropriating and collecting of created things, people have been led so far from God that they have forgotten the Creator.[9] They have even raised up and honored as gods the created things which had been made subject to them.[10] That is still the case for those who depart from God's order and forsake what God has ordained.

Now as has been said, however, created things which are too high for people to grasp and collect, such as the sun, the whole course of the heavens, day, air, and so forth, show that not only they, but also all other created things, were made common for all people.[11] Because they are too great to be brought under human control, they have remained common, and humans have not possessed them. Otherwise, since people had become so evil through wrongful acquisitions, they would also have wrongfully taken possession of such things and made them their own.[12]

It is therefore true that the rest is likewise not made by God for anyone's private possession. This is shown in that people must forsake all other created things as well as the high things when they die, and carry nothing with them as their own.[13] For this reason Christ counts all temporal things as alien to people's true nature and says, "If you have not been faithful with other people's property, who will entrust you with property of your own?"[14]

Because what is temporal is not ours but is alien to our true nature, the law commands that no one should covet someone else's possessions,[15] that is, set his heart upon them or claim them as his own.[16] Therefore, whoever will adhere unwaveringly to Christ and follow him must give up acquiring things and holding property.[17] Christ himself says,

---

Whoever will adhere unwaveringly to Christ and follow him must give up acquiring things and holding property.

"None of you can become my disciple if you do not give up all your possessions."[18] Whoever is to be renewed into the likeness of God must abandon what leads away from God, that is, grasping and collecting material possessions. Otherwise, God's likeness cannot be attained.[19] That is why Christ says, "Whoever does not receive the kingdom of God as a little child shall not enter it."[20] Christ also says, "Unless you overcome yourselves and become as little children, you shall not enter the kingdom of heaven."[21]

Whoever has become free from created things can then grasp what is true and divine. When the true and the divine become one's treasure, the heart turns toward that treasure, emptying itself from everything else[22] and regarding nothing any longer as its own but as belonging to all God's children.[23] Therefore, we say that as all believers share spiritual gifts,[24] still more should

---

Peter Riedemann (1506–1556) served as elder of the Hutterian communities in Moravia. This article is taken from his Hutterite Confession of Faith, *ed. John Friesen (Plough, 2019).*

they express this in material things and not covet or claim them for themselves, for they are not their own.[25] They will honor God, show that they partake in the fellowship of Christ,[26] and be renewed into God's likeness.[27] The more a person is attached to property and claims ownership of things, the further away he is from the fellowship of Christ and from being in the image of God.[28]

For this reason, when the church came into being, the Holy Spirit reestablished such community in a wonderful way. "No one said any of the things they possessed were their own, but they had all things in common."[29] This admonition by the Spirit is true for us even today. In the words of Paul, "Let each one look not to your own interests but to the interests of others." In other words, "Let each one look not to what benefits yourself, but to what benefits many."[30] Where this is not the case, it is a blemish upon the church that should

truly be corrected. Someone may say that this only applies to what took place in Jerusalem and therefore does not apply today. In reply, we say that even if it did only happen in Jerusalem,[31] it does not follow that it should not happen now. The apostles and the churches were not at fault, but the opportunity, the right means, and the right time were lacking.

This, therefore, should never be a reason for us to hesitate. Instead, it should move us to greater and better effort, for the Lord now gives us both the time and the occasion. It was not the fault of either the apostles or the churches, as is shown by the ardent efforts of both. The apostles directed people to the church with great diligence and spared no pains to teach them true surrender, as all their epistles still prove today.[32]

The people, especially those from Macedonia, obeyed with all their hearts, as Paul bears witness, saying, "I want to tell you of the grace given to the churches in Macedonia. Their joy was most abundant since they had been confirmed through much suffering, and their poverty, though it was great indeed, overflowed as riches in simplicity. I can testify that they voluntarily gave according to their means and beyond their means. They begged us earnestly and insistently to allow them to share in the support of other believers. In this they exceeded our hopes, giving themselves first to the Lord and then also to us, by the will of God."[33]

On the basis of this, we can recognize that the churches favorably inclined their hearts to practice community and were willing and ready to do so, not only in spiritual but also in material things. They wished to follow Christ their Master, become like him, and be of one mind with him.[34] He went before us in this way and commanded us to follow him.[35]

1. 1 John 1:1–3   2. Rom. 1:16–17   3. Phil. 2:1–8; 1 Cor. 12:12–27   4. Acts 2:42–47; 4:32–37   5. 2 Cor. 8:7–15   6. Exod. 16:16–18   7. Gen. 1:26–29   8. Gen. 3:2–12   9. Rom. 1:18–25   10. Wisd. of Sol. 13:1–3; 15:14–19   11. Gen. 1:25–31   12. Gen. 3:2–6; 2 Esd. 3:4–7; 7:12–15; Rom. 5:12–14   13. 1 Tim. 6:6–9   14. Luke 16:9–13   15. Exod. 20:17; Deut. 5:21   16. Luke 16:11–12   17. Matt. 10:37–39; Mark 8:34–38; Luke 9:23–26   18. Luke 14:33   19. Eph. 4:20–32; Col. 3:1–11   20. Mark 10:15; Luke 18:17   21. Matt. 18:1–4   22. Luke 12:33–40   23. Acts 2:44–45; 4:32–37   24. 1 John 1:3   25. Luke 16:11–13   26. 1 Cor. 10:16   27. Eph. 4:22–24; Col. 3:1–10   28. Gen. 1:25–27   29. Acts 2:44–45; 4:32–37   30. Phil. 2:2–4   31. Acts 2:38–45; 4:32–37   32. Phil. 2:1–11; Rom. 14:7–8   33. 2 Cor. 8:1–5   34. Phil. 2:5–8   35. Matt. 10:22–25; Luke 14:33

BUSINESS REPLY MAIL
FIRST-CLASS MAIL   PERMIT NO. 65   BIG SANDY, TX

POSTAGE WILL BE PAID BY ADDRESSEE

PLOUGH PUBLISHING
PO BOX 8542
BIG SANDY TX 75755-9769

Saving the Commons

*As the Industrial Revolution took off,
William Cobbett rose in defense
of the cottage economy.*

JACK BELL

IN 1822, A JOURNALIST and radical named William Cobbett began a series of journeys by horseback through the countryside of southern England. His aim, he declared, was "not to see inns and turn-pike roads, but to see the country; to see the farmers at home, and to see the labourers in the fields." To travel by turnpike – on the expanding network of toll roads designed to facilitate the commerce of goods destined for London – meant, he said, that you would "know nothing of England." Instead, by crossing fields, commons, or the narrow lanes used by farmers and workers, you could see the people of England "without any disguise or affectation."

Often traveling alone, Cobbett sought the most obscure pathways he could find, frequently going miles out of his way to avoid the smooth, newly constructed turnpikes he loathed. From his wanderings emerged *Rural Rides*, a wide-ranging sketch of rural life at the dawn of the Industrial Revolution. *Rural Rides* is a classic of nineteenth-century social criticism, pioneering new forms of travel and landscape writing; it was beloved by thinkers as different as Karl Marx and G. K. Chesterton. In the twenty-first century, it's largely forgotten outside academic circles. But Cobbett's critiques of enclosure make *Rural Rides* seem anything but dated.

From the early Middle Ages, the rural laboring classes in England had raised crops and livestock for their own personal use, even when they were not owners of the land they used. Access to this land was protected in different ways, and none more significant than the so-called rights of the common. Customs varied from village to village, but the rights of the common granted peasants (and later, the rural laboring classes) access to land for very specific purposes: to graze animals like cattle, sheep, and pigs; to harvest wild food and timber; to make hay; to glean after harvest; or to grow crops in very small allotments. The land might belong to a noble family, but those who lived on or near it had rights that the landowners and farmers were not supposed to interfere with. In many cases, the land peasants used was considered "waste," or land that wasn't tillable or worth improving.

In the late eighteenth century, workers' access to common resources came under attack. Numerous tracts of common and waste land were "enclosed" for tillage and grazing large flocks of sheep: rural families were forced off the land and their access to resources was severely curtailed. Modern agriculturalists like Arthur Young had promised landed English farmers increased capacity and higher yields through enclosure and monocropping. Following this cue, many landowners and farmers sought ways to absorb common and waste lands into their own agricultural holdings. Parliament assisted these efforts: from 1750 to 1850, it passed five thousand acts that restricted rural workers' access to what had been common resources. London banks provided the loans

---

Jack Bell farms with his family in the Piedmont region of North Carolina. He has taught literature at Wake Forest and Duke Universities and the University of Richmond.

Previous page: John Constable, *Ploughing Scene in Suffolk*, oil on canvas, ca. 1825 (detail).

necessary to clear the land of laborers and wildlife and grow crops; the new laws let owners do so. In some instances, the land was simply annexed without parliamentary consent. One estimate suggests that by the middle of the twentieth century, nearly one-fifth of England's land mass had transitioned from common to private use.

For farmers and landowners, enclosure was often a financial windfall. For those who lived and worked on the land, enclosure was a catastrophe. Although there were multiple forces conspiring against rural workers, enclosure amounted to what the economic anthropologist Karl Polanyi called "a revolution of the rich against the poor." Cobbett himself described it as a "shutting out of the labourers from all share in the land," forbidding them to even "look at a wild animal, almost at a lark or a frog." Enclosure was an ecological disaster too. Landowners who took possession of commons would tear down hedgerows, fill in ditches, drain ponds, and raze forests. With the natural biodiversity of the commons destroyed, farmers grew cash crops like wheat or barley on what remained. And enclosure imposed dire legal consequences on the hunting and foraging rural people had tacitly agreed upon for generations, destroying long-established customary arrangements of give-and-take that had supported the rural community.

Rural Rides documents the social consequences of enclosure and the centralization of agriculture. It tells us of workers' habits of dress, the state of their farms, the condition of the cottages they lived in. It also describes how enormous damage to the natural world impoverished the people who depended upon it. Long before more recent calls to return to indigenous methods of agriculture and land stewardship, Cobbett perceived the significance of farming with nature rather than against it: hedge-laying, tree-planting, coppicing, and other aspects of mixed, small-scale agriculture. This long-standing cottage economy not only encouraged enclaves of wildness in a landscape dominated by increasingly centralized agricultural systems, it had long helped the rural poor avoid dependence on parish relief or the chance of having a benevolent landlord. Cobbett called for his country's ruling classes to give back the common land they had stolen from their own people.

Cobbett was politically radical and theologically prescient. *Rural Rides* expresses the view of a world where the land is a common inheritance for all, not the property of a few. In an era where the systems of centralization and control Cobbett critiqued have led to an ecological crisis of existential proportions, we would do well to reconsider *Rural Rides*'s vehement critique of a system incapable of recognizing moral or environmental limits.

WILLIAM COBBETT was born in 1763 in the village of Farnham in Surrey, a place where, he would later write, "all is a garden." His father was a farmer. Cobbett would recall that his earliest memory of work was "driving the small birds from the turnip-seed, and the rooks from the peas." Intriguingly, Cobbett spent the first half of his life actively seeking to become a landowning farmer. As a young man, he worked for his father and on neighboring farms until in 1783 he mysteriously left home for London. Having learned to read and write on the farm, he found work as an attorney's clerk before another change of heart, joining the Royal Marines in 1784. In 1791 he was honorably discharged and, after marrying in 1792, set sail for America. Once across the Atlantic, he established a new career as an anti-American pamphleteer, writing under the pseudonym "Peter Porcupine."

How did an orthodox Tory become a relentless critic of Crown and Parliament and a champion of the rural poor? As Raymond Williams points out, when Cobbett finally returned to England after fifteen years abroad, he had earned "a reputation . . . as one of the most vigorous, indeed virulent, anti-democratic journalists" of the day.

John Constable, *Stour Valley and Dedham Church*, oil on canvas, ca. 1815 (detail)

Yet "within five years he is a radical; within ten in jail for sedition." Cobbett's road to radicalism began with the fulfillment of a lifelong dream. In 1805, he finally became a landowner.

After their return from America, Cobbett relocated his family to Botley, in Hampshire, where he purchased a farm. But soon afterward, a small parcel of land nearby (some common land, some waste) prompted a local political crisis. Farmers in the area wished to enclose the land, but they ran into stiff opposition – not least from Cobbett himself.

The nearly thirty smallholdings at Horton Heath raised sheep, cattle, poultry, hogs, and bees; cut firewood; and tended gardens in the midst of apple orchards and cherry trees. By Cobbett's estimate, these people "produced as much for themselves and for the market [on 150 acres of common and waste land] as any neighboring two-hundred-acre farm." What impressed Cobbett most was that they did this on land that was entirely "unimproved" by contemporary agricultural-reform standards. Cobbett proposed to other local landowners that each family should retain a small parcel of land. His fellow farmers rejected this, because they saw the smallholders' independence as a school for insolence and an inevitable financial drain on the parish. Cobbett's proposal was defeated. Soon after, Horton Heath was enclosed and its tenants expelled. It was a defining moment in Cobbett's life. From then until his death in 1835, he made the cause of the rural and urban poor his own.

THE POLITICS of enclosure would provoke Cobbett's journalistic ire for the rest of his life. Beneath the politics, Cobbett perceived a root cause: the failure of elites to acknowledge the thrift, productivity, and resilience of the cottage economy. Indeed, *Rural Rides* was a success because Cobbett was able to marry political critique with a fresh vision of the agricultural landscape and its people. He often begins by noticing and describing ordinary things: the quality of the turnips in a field, the vigor of hop plants twisting up their poles, the condition of a flock of snow-white ewes grazing in wheat stubble. It's a practical attention rooted in a love for the subtle variations of place – even ordinary and familiar ones.

Soils are Cobbett's favorite places to begin. At Hascombe Beech in Surrey, for instance, the ground is "a beautiful loam upon a bed of sand.

Cobbett begins by noticing and describing ordinary things: the quality of the turnips in a field; the vigor of hop plants twisting up their poles; the condition of a flock of snow-white ewes grazing in wheat stubble.

Springs start here and there at the feet of the hills, and little rivulets pour away in all directions." On the way from Winchester to Burghclere, in Hampshire, the soil is transformed into a "coverlet of flints upon a bed of chalk" before giving way to a "high, chalk bottom, open downs or large fields, with here and there a *farm-house in a dell*, sheltered by lofty trees, which, to my taste, is the most pleasant situation in the world." The hills from Hindhead to Blackdown (outside Guildford, Surrey) look like boiling copper in a pot "if you could, by word of command, *make it be still*." He is captivated by the "hangers" of the East Hampshire Hills, not far from where he was born ("never, in all my life, was I surprised and so delighted"). There, "the trees and underwood *hang*, in some sort, to the ground," Cobbett noted, "instead of *standing on* it." Many of these hangers remain, and you can still find the paths by them that Cobbett himself likely used.

Cobbett's eye for detail wasn't confined to the agricultural features of a landscape. He delights in what the poet Jeremy Hooker calls "ditch vision," the ability to spot wild things in ordinary and domesticated places. Crisscrossing the pastures and crops around Everley, in Wiltshire, Cobbett can't help but bring himself back to a "clump of lofty sycamores" in which resides "a most populous rookery, in which, of all things in the world, I delight." These interludes of wildness are thrilling to him. Many times, Cobbett's observational pleasures place the reader right alongside him as he puts pen to paper: "I am now sitting at one of the southern windows of this inn, looking across the garden towards the rookery. It is nearly sun-setting; the rooks are skimming and curving over the tops of the trees; while, under the branches, I see a flock of several hundred sheep

coming nibbling their way in from the Down, and going to their fold." On one journey, Cobbett is surprised by thousands of goldfinches picking their way through the thistle that lines the path in front of him. The thistle in the field has been hauled away with the hay crop, so the birds flock to seedheads growing unmown along the road. They stay beside him for half a mile until they move off as one.

For Cobbett, these little enclaves of wildness weren't just aesthetically remarkable; they had political significance. A few days into his first rural ride, he notices that the most prosperous laborers live in places where tillage agriculture hasn't destroyed old forests and hedgerows. The wildness of the land and the welfare of the rural poor were inseparably linked. Destroy the wild places, and you destroy the livelihood of the people living there. Let wild places thrive, and those people will thrive too. It's a kind of law in *Rural Rides* that "the more purely a corn country, the more miserable the labourers." ("Corn country" has been turned over solely to the production of grain.) In Thanet, a fertile peninsula that he describes as "ten square miles of corn," Cobbett makes his case. In such places "the great big bull frog grasps all. In this beautiful island every inch of land is appropriated by the rich. No hedges, no ditches, no commons, no grassy lanes: a country divided into great farms; a few trees surround the great farmhouse. All the rest is bare of trees; and the wretched labourer has not a stick of wood, and has no place for a pig or cow to graze, or even to lie down upon." Cobbett's point is both ecological and social. Enclosure and agricultural "improvement," he saw, suppressed the vitality of the land. It also suppressed the people who tended and kept it. Cobbett observes that in places where ponds have been turned into cropland, wild waterfowl are nowhere to be found. And he laments the clear decline in the habitat of wild rabbits: woods, hedges, the edges of fields. These ecological losses carry social consequences:

John Constable, *Dedham Vale, with a View to Langham Church from the Fields
Just East of Vale Farm, East Bergholt*, oil on canvas, ca. 1815

rural people no longer have access to traditional food sources over winter.

According to Cobbett, the promises of agricultural "progress" could be debunked by simply looking at the cottage economies of people who inhabited "unimproved" land. For example, he notes that the wildest, least-improved places yielded the best livestock and provided inhabitants a dependable source of income. "How curious is the natural economy of a country!" Cobbett remarks upon passing through the supposedly "wretched tracts" of Romney Marsh in Kent. The wastes, heaths, and commons of this place – "unspoilt (so far) from the touches of the Wen" – are unimproved. (A wen is an unsightly facial cyst, and it was Cobbett's preferred description of the conurbations that swelled around London.) And yet, Cobbett notes, "wastes" like the Fen country produce the fattest cattle he can find anywhere in England. The problem is that enclosure threatened to wipe away such realities from the face of the earth. Destroy the natural landscape, and the memory of the way of life that landscape sustained disappears forever.

This insight led Cobbett to an impassioned defense of traditional rural crafts. He wrote one of the first studies in agroforestry, *The Woodlands*. Another book, *The Cottage Economy*, sought to revive crafts like brewing, baking, gardening, and pig butchery. These concerns have an oddly contemporary air: agroforestry, the incorporation of tree crops with more traditional forms of agriculture, is a booming field. Gardening and homesteading are suddenly popular again.

John Constable, *The Wheat Field*, oil on canvas, 1816

OBBETT WAS MORE than a pioneer in ecological activism. Driving his politics is an account of creation that denies any human pretension to absolute ownership:

> The land, the trees, the fruits, the herbage, the roots are, by the law of nature, the common possession of all the people. . . . And, if a contingency arise, in which men . . . are unable, by moderate labour . . . to obtain food sufficient for themselves and their women and children, there is no longer *benefit* and *protection* to the whole; the social compact is at an end, and men have a right, thenceforward, to act agreeably to the laws of nature.

For Cobbett, these "laws of nature" have revolutionary implications. The divinely instituted bond between "all the people" and the creation they hold in common – "the land, the trees, the fruits, the herbage, and the roots" – has been severed, he implies, by the emergent capitalist order. In early industrial England, workers own neither land nor industry; neither the farmworker nor the factory hand is able to enjoy the fruits of his labor. Cobbett maintains that a robbery has taken place:

> Is a nation *richer* for the carrying away of the food from those who raise it, and giving it to bayonet men and others, who are assembled in great masses? I could broomstick the fellow who would look me in the face and call this "*an improvement.*" . . . [England] is the free-est country in the world; but, somehow or other, the produce is, at last, *carried away*; and it is eaten, for the main part, by those who do not work.

The criminals of England are not the starving poor who steal food they cannot afford, but the rich, who devise clever financial systems that siphon away food produced by laborers and sell it for a profit in the cities or abroad. Cobbett put these ideas to the test upon meeting a group of angry farmers on the road, intent on punishing an elderly man for stealing cabbages. "Would you punish a man, a poor man . . . and, moreover, an old man," Cobbett asks them, "when that Holy Bible, which I dare say you profess to believe in . . . teaches you that the hungry man may, without committing any offense at all, go into his neighbor's vineyard and eat his fill of grapes?" When the men insist that this fellow is a "bad man," Cobbett reminds them that "the Bible, in both Testaments, commands us to be merciful to the poor, to feed the hungry, to have compassion on the aged; and it makes no exception as to the 'character' of the parties."

DECADES AFTER Cobbett published *Rural Rides*, Karl Marx identified a rift in "the social-ecological metabolism" of the earth. Industrial capitalism, he argued, not only alienated the worker from his labor but also "hinder[ed] the operation of the eternal natural condition for the lasting fertility of the soil." In an industrial economy, agricultural products were consumed in the city. Once those products were consumed, how was a capitalist society supposed to return fertility to the soil? Trade, commerce, and the circulation of agricultural goods across long distances generated a "metabolic rift" between the country and the city. Marx predicted a looming agricultural catastrophe: eventually, capitalism would exhaust the fertility of the soil.

There is more than a little Cobbett in Marx's theory of a "metabolic rift." Marx was a great admirer of Cobbett; he described him as "the purest incarnation of Old England and the most audacious initiator of Young England. . . . As a

writer he has not been surpassed." For Marx, Cobbett was one of the few genuine revolutionaries of his generation. But Cobbett was revolutionary in the wrong direction, Marx thought: Cobbett wanted to turn the wheel of economic history backward, not forward. There's some truth to Marx's critique of Cobbett as a

We stand in desperate need of new ways of relating to the earth. Those new ways will no doubt include the dignity, thrift, and productivity of the cottage economy that Cobbett celebrated and practiced.

nostalgist: some of the old radical's opinions are reactionary or even racist, like his hatred of potatoes (they're from Ireland). But as the crisis Cobbett chronicled continues and acquires global proportions, with industrial agribusiness waging an unceasing war against nature, we stand in desperate need of new ways of relating to the earth. Those new ways will no doubt include the dignity, thrift, and productivity of the cottage economy that Cobbett celebrated in *Rural Rides* and which he himself practiced. In the end, Cobbett gestures toward the possibility that we might inhabit the earth without abusing it or each other; he contemplates how to take what we need for survival and possibly, if improbably, contribute to the flourishing of all the creatures with whom we share the natural world. In the kind of paradox Cobbett delighted in, the key to our future might very well lie in the wisdom of the past. ➤

On Owning Twenty-Two Cars

What is it like to live in a community where you possess nothing but share everything?

MAUREEN SWINGER

ONE COULD ARGUE that I own all twenty-two cars in the lot outside my house, as well as various vans, trucks, and two buses. So do the 260 other people at Fox Hill, the Bruderhof community where I live. Sharing all things in common is practical in a number of surprising ways, which is good because all members of our church community have taken a personal vow of poverty and don't own anything individually. For one thing, most of us work and

go to school on our communal premises, within easy walking or biking distance. We grow much of our own food, and a lot of the rest is purchased in bulk by a designated shopper. Many folk at Fox Hill may go days or even weeks without needing a car – or money, for that matter – at all.

So what happens when you do go on a trip, say, for a scheduled x-ray at the nearby hospital, or an outing to visit friends? You drop a note at the steward's office (preferably the day before your

Maureen Swinger is a senior editor at Plough. *She lives at the Fox Hill Bruderhof in Walden, New York, with her husband, Jason, and their three children.*

Photograph by Dave Morgan.

journey, emergencies excepted). Dave or Nick, who steward the vehicle fleet and the community funds, will set you up with the keys to a car that suits your needs. Party of six? Here's a minivan. Elderly? Something roomy with easier entry on the passenger side. Do you need a driver? They will find you one. Cash or credit card for a copay at the hospital, or for coffee or dinner with your friends? Here's an envelope that more than covers your request, and includes a small reminder to save your receipts and tally up your totals.

In a way it's similar to having your business pick up your work tab, but we've settled on this system for a higher reason than efficiency. We're accountable with funds and (hopefully) frugal in our spending because taking more than our fair share of the goods of the earth is not consistent with our beliefs. As stated in the Bruderhof's *Foundations of our Faith and Calling*, this vow of poverty is part of "gladly renouncing all private property, personal claims, and worldly attachments and honors."

All able-bodied members work, but any earnings belong to everyone, whether that work is on or off the community. Those who work for an outside employer direct their salaries to the central coffer; members who live in smaller urban communities might work in construction or health care. The rest of us contribute our labor to various community affairs: teaching in the schools, caring for the sick, growing and preparing food, and yes, writing and editing for the publishing house. Much of the community's revenue comes from the woodworking and medical equipment manufacturing businesses in which many members spend much of their working day.

But no matter which of these professions we participate in, none of us gets paid, and each of us is committed to being accountable. I doubt Nick or Dave has the time to scan every returned receipt, much less give feedback about it, though

of course they are obligated to bring up concerns if funds are misspent. To me, accountability is simply a reminder to myself that I'm part of a bigger family; my actions, including spending, affect the whole. (It's much the same with clothing, hobbies, or home decor; beyond the items we make ourselves, the onus is on each of us to decide between needs and wants – and whether our yen for trends is really worth everyone else paying for it.)

It's considered common courtesy to make sure your car is returned clean. The shed by the parking lot is home to a pressure washer and industrial vacuum system (as well as car seats of every conceivable size). Also, no car should be sitting there with less than half a tank of gas, and to that end, each car key has its own gas card in an attached sleeve.

My husband, Jason, is not inclined toward lamentations and hand-wringing, but one thing that reliably sets him off is a car with muddy floor mats or a low tank. I once teased him that when he had his own vehicle it was never spotless and rarely tanked up, but he countered immediately with, "That was mine; these are ours. What if the next people to step inside are off to the hospital with a baby on the way?" And he was absolutely right. In these circumstances, love is a fitted-out car.

But it's also a shared laundry machine or lawn mower, a bike, a blender – anything a household might commonly invest in, only to use it a few times a week. It makes spiritual as well as practical sense to use these items communally.

How does this work with food? A level below our central dining hall, there's a common pantry where families can pick up freshly baked bread, brown eggs (thanks to Christopher, our chicken farmer), milk, butter, vegetables, the best home-made strawberry and apricot jam (at least that's what's in the cooler now), and other household basics from trash bags to tinfoil. Did I mention coffee? Franklin's ethically sourced "Hof Roast."

Beyond the one communal meal a day prepared by our dedicated cooks, much of what's freely available for family meals is homegrown or home-made. Having spent years cobbling together family dinners on a budget, I find this remarkable on a daily basis. But we do have a communal budget, and although our willing store-keepers will order in things beyond the staples, there's a common goal to "live simply that others may simply live" – my grandpa John's favorite slogan – mindful that much of the rest of the world is not so blessed, and anything we save might go to help hungrier people.

TAKING MONEY OUT of the picture turns any practical assistance into soul care. Nowhere is that more clearly illustrated than with medical support, as our family has had reason to rediscover: Last summer Jason was fielding at a friendly softball game in his usual high-energy way when he crashed into a tree. It sounds impossible to do, but he was running backwards to catch a high fly ball and didn't know how close he was to the treeline. He tripped over a root and was thrown against the tree trunk at full force; we all saw his head snap forward, and then he was out cold. Before I could even get to him, three of his friends converged, two of them para-medics. They kept him still while others ran for a backboard and neck brace, and before the ambulance arrived he was stably strapped in. He woke up to see a support team gathered closely round, while my sensible daughter and a friend ran home to gather hospital essentials. Our minister said a prayer as the gurney rolled up, and we could see the rest of the game spectators praying too.

On the way in, Jason's primary care doctor (and fellow member), Jake, called me to give further instructions which I strove to hear over the ambulance siren. He stayed in touch through ER intake, walking us through tests we should request and advocating with the hospital staff; I was not left alone to try to make calm judgment calls while praying down my panic against paralysis or worse. Jason was horizontal for weeks with intense spinal pain, and Jake showed up every day to figure out the best medication and treatment, consulting with specialists and therapists till he was up and running again (though not in softball).

Meanwhile, even without the help of a tree I was starting to experience some symptoms of my own: severe joint pain, exhaustion, and general clunkiness. Turned out to be rheumatoid arthritis, an affliction I had not considered at all except perhaps in association with aging sailors. Like Jake, my doctor Anneke wouldn't quit till things were figured out. She continues to check in frequently as life goes forward, albeit at a new speed (or lack thereof). Had we been an isolated household, either of these episodes could have devastated not only our health but also our finances and employment.

I think of the community nurses who do prenatal and baby-care home visits, including showing up on a Saturday evening when that baby has an earache. Of how they cover surgical recovery or end-of-life care for our elderly. Their work is love, as they aren't earning a cent more than the ninety-year-old they are caring for.

SOME DAYS I DO MISS carrying a credit card on me; I miss the buzz of gratification that comes along with an impulse buy. (I don't miss the regret that frequently follows right after.) But those days are rare. With each year, it becomes clearer to me why I live this way. It's not just for security, although yes, there is peace in the knowledge that I am not living one health catastrophe away from ruin, or worrying about student loans or mortgages.

God has provided us an extended family who try to love and care for each other without letting dollar bills get in the way. It's a big family, and so I am rich. ⇘

Tom Badley, *Dollar Wave*, giclée on paper, 2016

Where Your Treasure Is

Readings from Nicolai Berdyaev, Basil of Caesarea, Maria Skobtsova, C. S. Lewis, and Dorothy Day

Artwork by Tom Badley

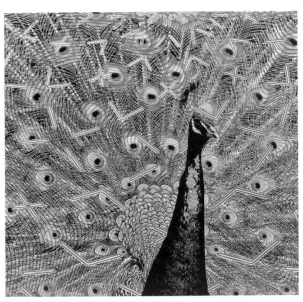

Tom Badley, *Peacock Study*, digital sketch, 2014

Nicolai Berdyaev

Nicolai Berdyaev (1874–1948) was a Russian Orthodox philosopher.

CHRISTIAN PIETY all too often has seemed to be the withdrawal from the world and from men, a sort of transcendent egoism, the unwillingness to share the suffering of the world and man. It was not sufficiently infused with Christian love and mercy. It lacked human warmth. And the world has risen in protest against this sort of piety, as a refined form of egoism, as indifference to the world's sorrow. Against this protest only a reborn piety can stand. Care for the life of another, even material, bodily care, is spiritual in essence. Bread for myself is a material question: bread for my neighbor is a spiritual question.

Source: Nicolas Berdyaev, *The Fate of Man in the Modern World*, trans. Donald A. Lowrie (London: SCM Press, 1935), 123–124.

About the artist: Tom Badley belongs to a small group of designers who work in the banknote industry – designing and printing physical money for central banks. Tom uses these same design processes in his work. He explains: "The pattern generation, the typography, the 'engraving' style, and the anatomy of the design itself – every element has been built from the expertise gained from a niche and secretive part of the printing industry – the part that happens to uphold the trust in our financial system.

"What is money? Money is love, fear, greed, life . . . money is the mirror of humanity. I've had a lifelong interest in art and money. The two were always inseparable for me. Art is a way of doing things and money permits things to be done – they are elemental in our world. I use art as a way of meditating on value, trust, and human potential." For more of his work go to *www.tombadley.net*.

Tom Badley, *HODL #7*, NFT, 2019

Basil of Caesarea

Basil of Caesarea (330–379) was a fourth-century bishop. Here he preaches on the story of the rich young man (Mark 10:17–31).

IF A PHYSICIAN PROMISED to cure some bodily defect, arising either from birth or as a result of illness, you would not lose heart. But when the Great Physician of souls and bodies, seeing your deficiency in this vital area, wishes to make you whole, you do not accept the joyful news, but rather turn sad and gloomy. . . .

If you had truly loved your neighbor, it would have occurred to you long ago to divest yourself of this wealth. But now your possessions are more a part of you than the members of your own body, and separation from them is as painful as the amputation of one of your limbs. Had you clothed the naked, had you given your bread to the hungry, had your door been open to every stranger, had you been a parent to the orphan, had you made the suffering of every helpless person your own, what money would you have left, the loss of which to grieve? Had you determined long ago to give to those in need, how would it be unbearable now to distribute whatever was left? At festival time, people do not regret parting with what they have at hand in order to gain whatever is necessary for the feast; rather, the cheaper they are able to purchase valuable commodities, the more they rejoice at receiving such a bargain. But you lament at relinquishing gold and silver and property – that is, stones and dust – in order to obtain the blessed life.

Source: Saint Basil the Great, *On Social Justice,* trans. C. Paul Schroeder (Saint Vladimir's Seminary Press, 2009), 43–44.

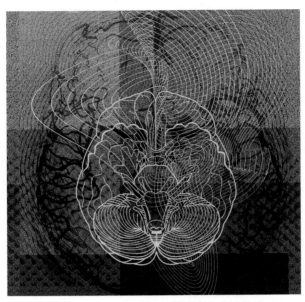

Tom Badley, *Inspiration, Version X*, giclée on paper, 2016

Maria Skobtsova

Mother Maria Skobtsova (1891–1945) was a nun who sheltered Jews and served the poor in Paris. She was killed in a Nazi concentration camp during World War II.

ACCORDING TO THE LAWS of matter, I must accept that if I give away a piece of bread, then I became poorer by one piece of bread. If I give away a certain sum of money, then I have reduced my funds by that amount. Extending this law, the world thinks that if I give my love, I am impoverished by that amount of love, and if I give up my soul, then I am utterly ruined, for there is nothing left of me to save. In this area, however, the laws of spiritual life are the exact opposite of the laws of the material world. According to spiritual law, every spiritual treasure given away not only returns to the giver like a whole and unbroken ruble given to a beggar, but it grows and becomes more valuable.

He who gives, acquires, and he who becomes poor, becomes rich. We give away our human riches and in return we receive much greater gifts from God, while he who gives away his human soul, receives in return eternal bliss, the divine gift of possessing the kingdom of heaven, How does he receive that gift? By absenting himself from Christ in an act of the uttermost self-renunciation and love, he offers himself to others. If this is indeed an act of Christian love, if this self-renunciation is genuine, then he meets Christ himself face to face in the one to whom he offers himself.

Source: Historical Studies of the Russian Church Abroad, copyright © 2008–2023. Used by permission.

Tom Badley, *Certificate of Authenticity*, giclée on paper, 2020

C. S. Lewis

C. S. Lewis (1898–1963) was a British novelist, poet,
and Christian apologist.

THERE IS ONE BIT OF ADVICE given to us by the ancient heathen Greeks, and by the Jews in the Old Testament, and by the great Christian teachers of the Middle Ages, which the modern economic system has completely disobeyed. All these people told us not to lend money at interest: and lending money at interest – what we call investment – is the basis of our whole system. Now it may not absolutely follow that we are wrong. Some people say that when Moses and Aristotle and the Christians agreed in forbidding interest (or "usury" as they called it), they could not foresee the joint stock company, and were only dunking of the private moneylender, and that, therefore, we need not bother about what they said.

That is a question I cannot decide on. I am not an economist and I simply do not know whether the investment system is responsible for the state we are in or not. This is where we want the Christian economist. But I should not have been honest if I had not told you that three great civilizations had agreed (or so it seems at first sight) in condemning the very thing on which we have based our whole life.

Source: C. S. Lewis, *Mere Christianity* (London: William Collins, 1952). Extract reprinted by permission.

Tom Badley, *Vergissmeinnicht*, giclée on paper, 2020

Dorothy Day

Dorothy Day (1897–1980) was an American writer, social activist,
and cofounder of the Catholic Worker Movement.

YES, THE POOR we are always going to have with us, our Lord told us that, and there will always be a need for our sharing, for stripping ourselves to help others. It always will be a lifetime job. But I am sure that God did not intend that there be so many poor. The class structure is of our making and our consent, not His. It is the way we have arranged it, and so it is up to us to change it. So we are urging revolutionary change. . . .

To attack poverty by preaching voluntary poverty seems like madness. But again, it is direct action. . . . To be profligate in our love and generosity, spontaneous, to cut all the red tape of bureaucracy! The more you give away, the more the Lord will give you to give. It is a growth in faith. It is the attitude of the man whose life of common sense and faith is integrated. To live with generosity in times of crisis is only common sense. ➵

Source: Dorothy Day, *The Catholic Worker*, 45:6, July 1, 1979 and *The Catholic Worker*, 31:2, September 1, 1964. Catholic News Archive, Catholic Research Resources Alliance, *thecatholicnewsarchive.org*. Used by permission.

Editors' Picks

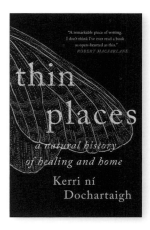

Thin Places
A Natural History of Healing and Home

By Kerri ní Dochartaigh (Canongate, 280 pages)

A "thin place," according to Kerri ní Dochartaigh, is explicitly Irish. It is a place where the curtain between what is known and unknown loosens, unfolds, and for a moment, disappears. Thin places are liminal, surprising, sacred, just as common in parking lots as in forests, "brimming with something like renewal." Many know this Celtic understanding as a way of seeing a beautiful, mystical order in the world, and ní Dochartaigh obliges: she follows birds on coast-lines, watches moths take flight, and listens as Ireland's habitats "sing of all that came and left, of all that is still here and all that is yet to come."

But for ní Dochartaigh, her native Ireland offers more than a token sense of generic mysticism. Ireland – and in particular, her childhood home of Derry – is a world made alive by violence, and especially the sectarian violence of her childhood that added more scars to Ireland's psyche and landscape. The conflict between Catholics and Protestants turned ní Dochartaigh's hometown into a place often made thin by gunshots in the streets. Ní Dochartaigh's own home was bombed when she was eleven, and the constant suspicion of locals toward her parents (one Catholic, one Protestant) meant that she spent her childhood in flight, her family constantly looking for safety as they fled housing complex after housing complex, teenage boys staring malevolently into their yard.

But ní Dochartaigh's book is more than a scrapbook of the violence that punctuated her early years. It is a pilgrimage through her inner and outer landscapes, along the River Foyle, the waterway that gave troubled Ireland its own liminal boundary, whose slippery surface sat nearby wherever she lived. She leaves Ireland as an adult, but what doesn't leave her is the pain, her body having kept score of the traumas of a broken family in a broken country. "Witnessing violence of the kind we did," she writes, "so often, so intimately, to such a destructive end – does something to you . . . you have too much weight around your neck."

Readers will need to be aware that much of this book chronicles ní Dochartaigh's reckoning with suicidal ideation and alcoholism. It is her honest reckoning with what she carries as a child of civil war. She also carries talismans of the natural world: rocks from the Foyle's banks, bird feathers, pebbles smoothed by water and wind.

Ní Dochartaigh returns to Ireland to keen, to wail, and to mourn; in doing so, she hears "a call back to the land that made me, that wounded and broke me, the land that turned out to be the only place that held the power for me to heal." It is this return, and her record of it, that could help us cross our own thresholds, or at least find room to "imagine what lies beyond the here and now."

—Allison Backous Troy, a writer and educator living in Grand Junction, Colorado

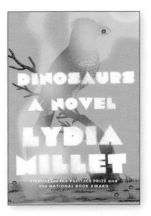

Dinosaurs
A Novel

*By Lydia Millet
(W. W. Norton, 240
pages)*

Gil, the protagonist of Lydia Millet's *Dinosaurs*, is a man who knows grief. Following the end of a relationship that had long been in the process of breaking down, he purchases a house sight-unseen in Arizona and walks to it from New York. He dubs his new home "the castle." It has high ceilings and large rooms.

> Perhaps Gil and his friends are the dinosaurs, forging a community destined to die out in a fragmenting landscape. Or perhaps they are the birds who adapt and survive and thrive.

He lives there alone, having been orphaned at the age of two and passed between guardians until inheriting his family's fortune at eighteen. His walk takes five solitary months. It is time he can take off, since "he had nowhere to be and no one who needed him."

The house next door is made of glass and soon a family moves in. Gil is disconcerted by their lack of privacy, as he can clearly observe the mother, father, teenage daughter, and preteen son going about their lives. Soon, the mother, Ardis, brings over an ice-breaking pie, and all parties acknowledge the awkwardness of the glass house. And so, an unusual relationship between the households forms.

Through spare prose and careful observation of people, Millet portrays community as if it were a gem held to light: each turn catches a new angle and casts a previously unseen color. They share meals. A friendship forms between Gil and the son, Tom. Bullied as a child, Gil is the first to see the signs that Tom is going through his own school torment. The stories of Gil's friendships spill out beyond these two homes, too. They look back to Gil's bond with the foul-mouthed Navy SEAL, Van Alsten. In Arizona, Gil befriends a repressed fellow women's shelter volunteer, Jason, and a kind surgeon, Sarah.

Community, however, brings deep pain. *Dinosaurs* is not a misanthropic novel, but Millet remains clear-eyed about the failures of human beings to live well together. To be open to relationships may mean being used, as Gil is for his wealth, or abused, like the women at the shelter. To have a friend can lead to loss. To have neighbors can lead to having a Neighborhood Association. The 2016 American presidential election haunts the novel's backdrop, signaling a fracturing in American community from which it may not recover. Finally, humans fail to live in community with nature, as the quail, hawks, and hummingbirds Gil observes become victims of a neighborhood poacher.

Is there, then, any hope to be found in community? The title, *Dinosaurs*, looks back on those creatures that went extinct because they could not adapt to a world radically changed by catastrophe. Perhaps Gil and his friends are the dinosaurs, forging a community destined to die out in a fragmenting political and environmental landscape. Or perhaps they are the birds who adapt and survive and thrive. Either way, the book's concerns remain largely with the here and now, where grief forges a kind soul and every creature to the smallest bird is loved.

*—James Smoker, a PhD candidate at the University of
St Andrews School of Divinity, Scotland*

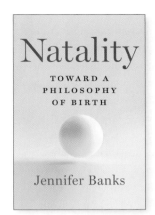

Natality
Toward a
Philosophy of Birth

Jennifer Banks
(W. W. Norton, 272
pages)

The German-born Jewish philosopher Hannah Arendt escaped a French internment camp with only a toothbrush to her name and what would become a surprisingly hopeful core tenet in her philosophy: natality. She writes, "Once called into existence, human life cannot turn into nothingness." What would it be like, wonders Jennifer Banks in her spectacular book *Natality*, if philosophy were more oriented toward the idea that, in Arendt's words, humans "are not born in order to die but in order to begin"? Banks draws into conversation with each other seven figures – Arendt, Friedrich Nietzsche, Mary Wollstonecraft, Mary Shelley, Sojourner Truth, Adrienne Rich, and Toni Morrison – who, each in his or her own way, deeply engages with the significance of birth.

Natality, Banks argues, bears little relationship to pronatalism; it is not about how many births there are but what it means that we are born at all. Arendt never had children and several of the figures Banks profiles are ambivalent about birth itself, one (Wollstonecraft) even ultimately dying of it. Radicalized by her own experience of childbirth, the feminist poet Adrienne Rich was eager to devour Arendt's writings, but witheringly critical of what she found. Arendt, with her focus on the possibilities of newness, dismisses maintenance labor: "the daily fight in which the human body is engaged to keep the world clean and prevent its decay bears little resemblance to heroic deeds; the endurance it needs to repair every day anew the waste of yesterday is not courage, and what makes the effort painful is not danger but its relentless repetition."

To Rich, this was obviously coded as women's work: "The million tiny stitches, the friction of the scrubbing brush, the scouring cloth, the iron across the shirt, the rubbing of cloth against itself to exorcise the stain, the renewal of the scorched pot, the rusted knifeblade, the invisible weaving of a frayed and threadbare family life" – that is, the many necessary tasks of caring for the humans one has brought into being – constitutes the "activity of world-protection, world-preservation, world-repair." Rich was no domestic goddess and did not find such work fulfilling in itself, but for that very reason recognized the stamina it took to face it down day after day. Though Arendt

> The miracle that saves the world, the realm of human affairs, from its normal, "natural" ruin is ultimately the fact of natality.

and Rich differ, they share an understanding that birth is what refutes, in Rich's words, the "deep fatalistic pessimism as to the possibility of change." Children, in an existential sense, reverse the entropy of human life. Writes Arendt: "The miracle that saves the world, the realm of human affairs, from its normal, 'natural' ruin is ultimately the fact of natality."

For Arendt, whether against entropy or evil, natality signifies faith and hope: "It is this faith in and hope for the world that found perhaps its most glorious and most succinct expression in the few words with which the gospels announced their 'glad tidings': 'A child has been born unto us.'"

—*Caitrin Keiper, editor-at-large of* Plough

HISTORY

ARRIVES ON THE

ISLAND

How should we write history?
An excerpt from a new novel.

EUGENE VODOLAZKIN

Translated from the Russian
by Lisa C. Hayden

*E*UGENE VODOLAZKIN'S *new novel* A History of the Island, *which* Plough *released in May, is presented as the chronicle of an island from medieval to modern times. The island is not on any map, but it is real beyond doubt. It cannot be found in history books, but the events will be recognizable. The chronicle has been newly annotated by an elderly couple, Parfeny and Ksenia, who are the island's former rulers. Here is the first chapter.*

LONG AGO, WE HAD NO HISTORY. Memory preserved isolated events, but only those events with a propensity for repeating. Our existence thus seemed to take a circular path.

We knew that night follows day and spring follows winter. The luminaries floating in the firmament create those circles and their wayfaring is limited to one year. The year was also the natural boundary of our memory.

We vaguely recalled dreadful hurricanes and earthquakes, fierce winters when the sea froze, and internecine wars and invasions of other tribes, but we could not specify when they were happening.

We said only: That happened one summer. Or: That happened in spring, many springs ago. And thus all hurricanes blended into one large hurricane and internecine wars became for us one unending war.

With Christianization, we heard the word of the Holy Scripture, though previously we heard only one another's shabby old words. Those words crumbled to dust, for only that which is written is preserved and we had no written language before Christianization.

Books arrived on the Island later and we then learned of events that occurred before us. This helped us to understand the events of today.

We know now that human history has a beginning and is hastening toward its end. With these thoughts in mind, we shall set about to describe the years and events that flow past.

Bless us, O Lord.

PARFENY:

Monks wrote *A History of the Island*. Nothing surprising there: only someone focused on eternity is capable of depicting time, and one who thinks of the celestial is the best person of all to understand the earthly. Time was different then, too: boggy, viscous. Not as it is these days. Time is slow during childhood, it lingers, but later it takes a running start and then, toward the end of life, it flies. That is pretty much common knowledge. Isn't the life of a people rather similar to the life of an individual person?

People suppose that the chronicle's first chapters are the work of Father Nifont the Historian. In the entire history of its existence, the manuscript never once left the walls of Island Monastery of the Savior. That was most strictly forbidden.

In the chroniclers' opinion, when a history was located within a

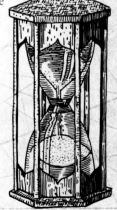

sacred space, it was protected from forgery. People handle a history more freely now: anyone at all, in any place, writes history. Might the reason for numerous falsifications lie there?

The prohibition on bringing the chronicle out of the monastery did not preclude the possibility of familiarizing oneself with it inside the monastery's walls. For the ruling princes, at any rate. It was thought (as now, too) that knowledge of the past is essential for those holding power. That notion seems fair to me. True, it is also fair to say that knowledge of history has yet to prevent anyone from making mistakes.

THE ISLAND WAS CHRISTIANIZED in the days of devout Prince Feodor. The prince was named Alexander until that time and not Feodor. And he was not devout. And he ruled only the northern part of the Island but seized the southern part during internecine war and became prince of the entire Island.

In the eighth year of his rule, he said:

Everyone gather on the Sandbank and you will be baptized there.

He said:

Whoever does not accept baptism is not my friend.

Everyone – or nearly everyone – was baptized, understanding that it is a difficult matter to not be a friend of the prince.

KSENIA:
According to Byzantine Emperor Justinian's *Novel 47*, historical events are dated based on the current length of the reign of the emperor in power. Following the Byzantine tradition, Nifont the Historian (as well as all subsequent chroniclers) dates events with the ordinal number denoting how many years the prince has reigned. As is commonly known, we did not have emperors.

THE GOSPEL WAS BROUGHT to the Island and read to people, and everyone learned of the life of our Lord Jesus Christ.

It was ascertained about old gods that they were wooden idols, that they did not need to be defended since if they were gods they would defend themselves. And nobody particularly clung to them beyond the few sorcerers who served them.

When the pagan gods were burned, sorcerers said the day would come when words in books would also burn. No one believed them since everyone thought they spoke from powerless malice. And also, perhaps, because they had never known written words. The words they uttered hung in the air until the next wind, when they were carried off.

In the twentieth year of Feodor's reign, historical books were sent to the Island. We store them most carefully: There is nothing worse than remaining without history at a time when you are only beginning to understand what history is. From those books we discovered that history is singular and universal and, even when it is mislaid on an unknown island, it is one branch of our common tree.

We also learned that history was predicted in prophecies that encompass both its entire whole and its minor parts. A prophecy surmounts time and thus opposes the ordering of time. The great prophet Elijah, who rose to the heavens in a fiery chariot, was freed by the Lord from death and

Eugene Vodolazkin, born in Kyiv, Ukraine, is one of Russia's leading novelists and an expert in medieval history and folklore. He lives with his family in St. Petersburg, where he works in the department of Old Russian Literature at Pushkin House.
Lisa C. Hayden is an award-winning translator and blogger. She lives in Maine.

time, which, when all is said and done, are one and the same.

The people of the Island have a prophet of their own, by the name of Agafon the Forward-Looking. He speaks according to inspiration, not according to books, for there are not yet books about the Island. He gives predictions covering a long period, thus there has yet to be an opportunity to verify them. Nonetheless, Agafon's way of thinking and overall degree of concentration speak to his forecasts coming true, so we place our trust in them. Particularly the prediction that the hostility wracking this piece of dry land will be broken for a long time when two princely lines come together as one.

I think enough has been said about prophecies. We will not delve deeply into the future and, remembering that history recounts the past, we shall return to what has already been stated.

PARFENY:

Agafon the Forward-Looking taught that a prophecy does not imply limitations to the freedom of future generations. It stands to reason that they, our descendants, are unrestricted in their actions insofar as circumstances allow. The reason for circumstances, says Agafon, is people, not God.

It is hard not to agree with him: long life has convinced me that people themselves create their own circumstances. Obviously, they are most often unfavorable. God sees them and reveals them to people through prophets. Sometimes.

And so, through Agafon, it was revealed to us when hostilities would break out on the Island. Nifont the Historian refers to that prophecy as not yet coming true. It is now known to all that it did come true. It was, so to say, a medium-term prophecy.

There was, however, one more of Agafon's prophecies that touched on distant times. It did not reach us. Unlike the others, which carried a more or less private character, this one was devoted to the fate of the Island in its entirety. Unfortunately, we haven't the slightest sense of its insights. Or perhaps that is

fortuitous, though that can only be decided after reading it.

Saint Agafon dictated his principal prophecy in the literal sense, into the ear of chronicler Prokopy the Nasal. Agafon, who by then had reached the age of one hundred and twenty, had very strictly forbidden the one writing to loosen his tongue. For Agafon's part, that of a person who was (if it may be expressed this way) of a mature age, this was a joke to some degree (after all, nobody prohibited saints from joking) since Prokopy's tongue was cut off for using foul language back in the years of his youth. One did not need to worry about asking him to hold his tongue.

Prokopy, however, acted unexpectedly, in a way that required no tongue. After taking apart the manuscript of the chronicle, he removed the prophecy and, according to rumor, secretly forwarded it to the mainland, to a likely (as people now say) adversary.

Prokopy's deed – if reports are true – suggests that the secret information did not look especially optimistic for Island residents. It's possible it could have somehow strengthened the aggressive designs of those on the continent – nothing raises an adversary's spirit like a prophecy received in a timely fashion.

The only possible way to pass judgment on Prokopy the Nasal's goals would be to familiarize

oneself with the prophecy's text but, as has been stated, it was lost without a trace. Why did he not rewrite it instead of pulling it out of the manuscript? After all, his action deprived his compatriots of the opportunity to read it.

It cannot be ruled out that the chronicler's actions aimed to exact revenge on his strict motherland for the loss of his tongue. That was an appreciable loss for Prokopy: the deceased loved to talk. He somehow contrived to do so using the bit that remained in his mouth. (A tongue, they say, grows back slightly.) Come what may, the story of the theft of the prophecy from the manuscript was discovered only after his death. This is striking evidence that people were not especially interested in the chronicle during Prokopy's time.

F I AM TO BE BRIEF, books brought to the Island have informed us of the following about the past.

On the first day, God created the heavens and the earth, the earth was unseen and unembellished, and the Spirit of God was moving over the waters, enlivening the watery essence. And God said, "Let there be light," and so there was light.

In the next days, He made the sea, rivers, and heavenly bodies. When filling the world with water, He left islands and lands in order to delineate dry ground before the creation of the sun, that people not deem the sun a god because it had dried the land.

God created fish and birds at the same time for they are akin, with but the difference that fish swim in water and birds in the sky.

And God created man and woman in order that he leave his mother and his father, and cleave to his wife. And God gave all earth's dry land to them to possess.

Seven days of creation, however, were still not time. Time was revealed at the Fall and the banishment from paradise, and history began together with time because history exists only within time.

At the age of 230, Adam sired his son Seth; all the years of Adam's life were 930. And children began to be born and from Adam to Noah there were counted ten generations and 1468 years. When Noah turned 600 years old, there was a flood on the earth.

And upon God's command, Noah struck a semantron and birds and beasts began to gather at the ark he had built, every creature in pairs, except the fish, for water did not frighten them. When all had entered, Noah closed the door to the ark and the windows of the heavens opened. And rain poured down for forty days and forty nights so there was no dry land left and even our island went under water. In the place where clouds now hang there were in those days rolling waves.

In one of the nonbiblical writings, it is said that the devil, wishing to sink the human race, transformed into a mouse and began to gnaw the bottom of the ark. Noah then prayed to God and a lion sneezed, releasing from his nostrils a tomcat and a she-cat, and they strangled the mouse. That is how cats, who are still a rarity in our land, came about.

PARFENY:

In Nifont's text we find apocryphal pieces of information that the modern reader will regard as steeped in legend: I have in mind the story of cats. The details, which show the difference between storytelling and Darwin's ponderous prose, are wonderful and all that is wonderful is true in some way.

And there it is: the origin of a species, without being dragged out over hundreds of pages. What can be seen clearly here are cats, and there you have them: flying out of a lion's nostrils, meowing as they flip in the air and land on four paws. Without forgetting their super-objective, they end up next to the mouse in one leap and then scritch-scratch! I say *scritch-scratch* because I have in mind that the duel was unusual to the highest degree. Did the cats know who they were up against? That's a good question.

It is true that these pieces of information do not fully correspond with Darwinism but that's more likely a problem with Darwinism. Its founder simply would not have understood the story about cats. It seems to me that he didn't know how to smile.

On a serious note. Given my considerable age, I am often asked about my attitude toward Darwin. What can I say? His ear that caught the rhythms of evolution turned out not to hear the pulse of metaphor and (more broadly speaking) poetry. Only Charles's inability to hear metaphor can explain his pouncing on the Holy Scripture. Only his insensitivity to poetry prevented him from understanding that he was not contradicting a biblical text. I think the deceased now understands that.

THE LORD GAVE WATER to us Island residents both to assist and to punish. Since time immemorial water has carried our cargo ships to distant corners of the inhabited world, to the line establishing the limit of sea and earth. But at the time of our spiritual devastation, water rose to a threatening height, drowning people and flooding fields. So said our forefathers. Given that the entire world was flooded with water, one can only be astounded by the degree that humans fell during Noah's time.

And on the fortieth day, Noah opened a window of the ark and sent forth a raven to learn where the water had receded. But the raven alit on dead bodies floating upon the water's surface, began pecking them, and did not return. And then Noah sent a dove. The dove returned, holding an olive branch in its beak, and Noah understood that the water had begun to subside.

Noah died 350 years after the flood; all the years of his life were 950.

KSENIA:

The unthinkable longevity of our forefathers might seem to some to be the result of a misunderstanding, perhaps an incorrect transposition from one chronological system to another, a scribe's error, etc. Strictly speaking, there is no need for these sorts of conjectures. Everything has an explanation.

People were still filled with a paradisiacal timelessness. Standing with one foot in eternity, they were still becoming accustomed to time. Their lifetime shortened as they became more distant from paradise. That said, one should not think that longevity ended with our forefathers. Parfeny and I are now three hundred forty-seven years old and that surprises no one.

Yesterday I answered a survey. In response to the question *What is your age?* I said: "Three hundred forty-seven."

They didn't even smile.

I used to feel shy about my age but that stopped after one hundred fifty. Some people simply live longer, for various reasons.

A History of the Island
Eugene Vodolazkin

"A masterpiece by one of Europe's finest contemporary novelists."
—Rowan Williams

"Eugene Vodolazkin has emerged in the eyes of many as the most important living Russian writer." —*New York Review of Books*

Hardcover, 320 pages, $26.95 $18.87 **with subscriber discount**

PLOUGH BOOKLIST

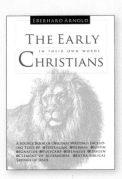

Christianity and Money

The Early Christians
In Their Own Words
Eberhard Arnold

In these firsthand accounts of the early church, the spirit of Pentecost burns with prophetic force through the fog that envelops the modern church. A clear and vibrant faith lives on in these writings, providing a guide for Christians today.

The Early Christians is a collection of primary sources on topics such as church and state, worship and church practices, creed and confession, proclamation and prophesy. It includes extra-biblical sayings of Jesus and excerpts from Origen, Tertullian, Polycarp, Clement of Alexandria, Justin, Irenaeus, and others. Equally revealing material from pagan contemporaries – critics, detractors and persecutors – is included as well.

Hardcover, 379 pages, $28.00 **$19.60 with subscriber discount**

The Reckless Way of Love
Notes on Following Jesus
Dorothy Day

In this guidebook Dorothy Day offers hard-earned wisdom and practical advice gained through decades of seeking to know Jesus and to follow his example and teachings in her own life.

Unlike larger collections and biographies, which cover her radical views, exceptional deeds, and amazing life story, this book focuses on a more personal dimension of her life: Where did she receive strength to stay true to her God-given calling despite her own doubts and inadequacies and the demands of an activist life? What was the unquenchable wellspring of her deep faith and her love for humanity?

Softcover, 149 pages, $12.00 **$8.40 with subscriber discount**

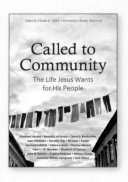

Called to Community
The Life Jesus Wants for His People
Edited by Charles E. Moore, Foreword by Stanley Hauerwas

Increasingly, Christians want to follow Christ together in daily life and share their lives more fully with others. As they take the plunge, they are discovering the rich, meaningful life that Jesus has in mind for all people, and pointing the church back to its original calling: to be a gathered, united community that demonstrates the transforming love of God.

Of course, community isn't easy. The selections in this volume are, by and large, written by practitioners – people who have pioneered life in intentional community and have discovered in the nitty-gritty of daily life what it takes to establish and sustain a Christian community over the long haul.

Softcover, 378 pages, $18.00 **$12.60 with subscriber discount**

Hudson Taylor

*"When I am a man, I mean to
be a missionary and go to China."*

MAUREEN SWINGER & SUSANNAH BLACK ROBERTS

THERE WAS ONLY one passenger aboard the clipper *Dumfries* when she set sail for China on September 19, 1853. The ship spent her first twelve days out of Liverpool caught in a violent storm in the Irish Sea, and almost foundered.

The passenger, Hudson Taylor, was a twenty-one-year-old, half-trained physician and entirely untrained missionary. Stowed in the cargo hold, he worried about his family and about the investment in his fare made by the newly-formed China Evangelical Society (CES) – money badly spent, if he should be lost at sea. "The Captain," he wrote later, "was calm and courageous, trusting in the Lord for his soul's salvation. The steward said he knew that he was nothing, but Christ was all. I felt

thankful for them, but I did pray earnestly that God would have mercy on us and spare us for the sake of the unconverted crew."

His mother had insisted he take a swimming-belt with him on the long sea voyage, but the young missionary felt that to wear it was to show a lack of trust in God. He gave it away to one of the clipper's crew. "I was," the passenger wrote later, "a very young believer, and had not sufficient faith in God to see Him in and through his use of means." In other words, it simply hadn't occurred to him that God might actually want to save him through his mother's foresight, and a bit of Victorian safety equipment. After he gave away the swimming-belt, "strange to say, I put several

---

Maureen Swinger and Susannah Black Roberts are senior editors at Plough.

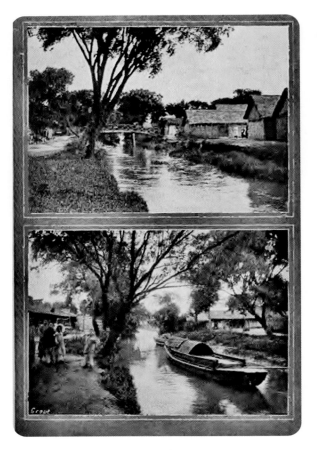

ONE DAY, DEEP IN PRAYER, he felt that call affirmed: "I felt I was in the presence of God, entering into covenant with the Almighty. I felt as though I wished to withdraw my promise, but could not. Something seemed to say 'Your prayer is answered, your conditions are accepted.' And from that time the conviction never left me that I was called to China."

By age eighteen, Taylor was studying Mandarin, training as a physician, and writing to mission boards to find a way of traveling to a nation that was, at that time, largely unknown to Europeans. The missionary movement, driven by a heartfelt sense of the obligations imposed upon all Christians by the Great Commission "to preach the gospel to every creature" was in full swing. Eventually Taylor found his way to the CES, which paid his fare, promised to support him on his arrival, and then sent him off into the storms of the Atlantic.

He arrived at Shanghai in the midst of another storm: this time, a political one. In 1842 the First Opium War ended in British victory. The Chinese empire's attempt to prevent British traders smuggling opium from India into China failed: the emperor was forced to consent to the humiliating Treaty of Nanking. It is known in China to this day as the first of the "Unequal Treaties." British warships kept their guns trained on Nanjing until the government agreed to sign the articles of the treaty, one of which opened five port cities to foreign trade. Another permitted foreign missionaries to live in the country. Neither clause was welcome to the Chinese government.

But even under the new treaty, much of China remained effectively closed to outsiders, and foreigners were left relying on rumors to make sense of the political and social turbulence wracking the empire. In 1850, three years before the *Dumfries* arrived in Shanghai, a self-proclaimed prophet in South China named Hong Xiuquan had declared himself the younger brother of Jesus

light things together, likely to float [if the ship went down], without any thought of inconsistency or scruple." This paradoxical attitude – casting himself entirely on God but being canny and intelligent in the way that he did so – was something of Hudson Taylor's hallmark.

In the event, the *Dumfries* did not go down, and five months later, her sole passenger landed safely at Shanghai.

It was a moment Taylor had dreamed of since 1837, when, as a child of five he told his parents, "When I am a man, I mean to be a missionary and go to China." After a powerful Evangelical conversion when he was a teenager, Taylor's conviction that he was being called to China only strengthened.

Hudson Taylor traveled by boat around the canals and waterways of China, preaching and distributing Bibles.

Christ. Denouncing China's ruling Qing dynasty as demonic, he established a new state – the "Heavenly Kingdom" – in opposition. Hong sought to convert China to his own syncretistic version of Christianity, a blend of Protestantism – gleaned from missionary tracts – Confucianism, Daoism, and Chinese folk religion, all of which had, he said, been revealed to him in visions.

Xiuquan's rebellion, often called the Taiping Rebellion, would leave 20 million dead. When Hudson Taylor arrived in Shanghai, the war had been fought for three years and would continue for eleven more.

Between the war, debilitating cold, lack of funds or long-term housing, and, despite his study of Mandarin, his inability to communicate with native speakers, Taylor's first year in Shanghai was daunting. Letters – and money from home – took months to arrive. Even as Taylor worked to help the CES understand conditions in Shanghai, he struggled to find inner peace: "Jesus is here, and though unknown to the majority and uncared for by many who might know Him, He is present and precious to His own."

While studying local dialects Taylor began preaching journeys up the Yangtze and Hwangpu Rivers, always accompanied by a more fluent missionary, a Chinese teacher, and a hired navigator, using houseboats to reach the more distant cities and islands. He often joined forces with another doctor, and together they combined preaching the gospel with care for the sick.

In many cases, the missionaries were met with great interest and keen curiosity. But they also found themselves threatened by crowds who suspected foreigners of aiding and abetting Xiuquan's rebellion (given their talk of Jesus), or of expanding the opium trade. On occasion, Taylor's group was attacked by soldiers from both sides of the conflict. Once they returned to see Shanghai in flames, besieged by the forces of the Heavenly Kingdom.

"I hope to go inland again in a few days," Taylor wrote to a colleague at one point. "You will join us in thanking the Lord for His protection in recent dangers. The Rebellion, especially since foreigners have enlisted themselves on both sides, has made access to the interior no easy matter. But the Word of God *must* go, and we must not be hindered by slight obstacles in the way of its dissemination."

REALIZING EARLY ON that his European dress and habits made him an object of suspicion, Taylor took up the clothing styles and food of his adopted country, to the disapproval of the staid British subjects in the "foreigners' compound" where he lived in Shanghai. But the missionary found that along with this decision, his relationships with people in China became deeper, his conversations about the gospel more

Hudson Taylor was careful never to suggest the gospel was the possession of Europeans.

thoughtful. Taylor would wear Chinese clothing for the rest of his life, and he asked this of his coworkers as well, as a gesture of respect for the culture that was hosting them.

In this attitude, Taylor was in sharp opposition to most missionaries of the day. Taylor was careful never to suggest the gospel was the possession of the English, or of Europeans: Christ loved all men and women in every country and showed no partiality. The English had converted because centuries before, unnamed missionaries had brought Christ's message to Britain's native Saxons and Celts. That flame of faith had, from Taylor's perspective, been renewed regularly in those islands, most recently in the preaching of John and Charles Wesley. Taylor's father had been a Methodist lay preacher, and although Taylor was himself a Baptist, his missionary work had an ecumenically Protestant basis.

Taylor's writings show reverence for the ancient culture in which he found himself, and reveal the love and honor in which he held its people. This sympathetic approach to Chinese culture,

> ## Taylor's writings show reverence for the ancient culture in which he found himself, and reveal the love and honor in which he held its people.

and Taylor's adoption of Chinese clothing, were frequently misunderstood and mocked by Europeans, including some who worked with him.

On one journey south to the city of Ningbo, he visited a small outpost of missionaries: there, he met the two daughters of Reverend Samuel Dyer. Dyer had been among the first missionaries in China, and had left his daughters orphans when they were very young. Maria, then age eighteen, and her sister were working as schoolteachers in Ningbo when Taylor arrived in the city. Maria was fluent in Mandarin and several other languages, wholeheartedly dedicated to mission work, and impatient with anything that smacked of security or privilege. The previous year, she had turned down the proposal of Sir Robert Hart, then serving as a diplomat with the British consulate. It was Taylor's first encounter with his future bride.

BY 1857, HE HAD MOVED south to Ningbo to found a mission hospital. Having severed ties with the Chinese Evangelical Society, he relied on prayer and the donations of friends in England. Several new Christians joined him, for which he was thankful, most notably Wang Laiquan, Feng Ninggui, Ni Yongfa, and Qiu Guogui: men who would be Taylor's most important colleagues for the work ahead. Whether supporting the hospital work or evangelizing through the city and later, the provinces, these four and soon others reached thousands in sharing their faith.

Ningbo brought Taylor into closer association with Maria Dyer; they were soon deeply in love. Maria's employer, the woman who ran the school, had little faith in Taylor's modus operandi of trust in God for all practical matters, with no safety net. Even Taylor doubted whether he should ask Maria to live so daringly, but she proved just as confident in God's providence as he.

She also proved a good bit more businesslike: when they married, she took up much of his administration and correspondence, while counseling and holding prayer meetings for women. And her linguistic ability, in major languages and in dialects, was exceptional: she was so fluent in Ningbo that she could translate English books into the dialect on the spot while teaching classes. With Maria, Taylor founded the China Inland Mission.

CIM grew, under Taylor's direction, gradually assuming responsibility for the work of eight hundred European missionaries and five hundred Chinese missionaries in all eighteen provinces. Together, the Taylors started 125 schools and 300 other stations of work, supporting various ministries including medical workers. Taylor eventually completed his own medical degree, and later recruited other doctors to the mission. Before his death in 1905, fifty-one years after that first landing, he saw 20,000 people come to Christ as the result of the China Inland Mission. He never lost his awareness of his calling: to offer Christ to anyone who would receive him. ➤